T0182517

HOW TO FIND PEACE

Living in a Challenging World

J KRISHNAMURTI

Edited by Frode Steen,
Douglas Evans, Duncan Toms

WATKINS
1893

How to Find Peace
J Krishnamurti

First published in the UK and USA 2024 by
Watkins, an imprint of Watkins Media Limited
Unit 11, Shepperton House, 89–93 Shepperton Road
London N1 3DF

enquiries@watkinspublishing.com

Design and typography copyright © Watkins Media
Limited 2024

Text Copyright © Krishnamurti Foundation of America
and Krishnamurti Foundation Trust 2024.

A CIP record for this book is available from
the British Library

ISBN: 978-1-78678-930-3 (hardback)
ISBN: 978-1-78678-931-0 (ebook)

1 3 5 7 9 10 8 6 4 2

Printed and bound by CPI Group (UK) Ltd, Croydon, CR0 4YY

ww.watkinspublishing.com

CONTENTS

ABOUT THIS BOOK

In 1992, the Krishnamurti Foundation of America was invited to join the World Future Society's (WFS) convention in Washington D.C. to share Krishnamurti's thoughts on the future of humanity.

Mr Milton Friedman, then a White House speechwriter, and trustee of the Foundation, suggested 'Social Responsibility' to title a compilation of Krishnamurti's work for this purpose. Foundation editors selected excerpts from a range of his teachings that emphasize that every individual must take responsibility for world change.

Social Responsibility was launched at the WFS convention and was provided to every attendee. Krishnamurti's challenge – to take responsibility for the state of the world and the corruption of consciousness – provided broad moral and ethical grounding for the exploration of the future of humanity.

Given the current situation in the world, from extreme political divisions to environmental destruction, to a multitude of wars and conflicts, the content remains highly relevant. The book has therefore now been expanded and re-edited with a new title for publication.

INTRODUCTION

Pacem in Terris

At its invitation, Krishnamurti spoke at the United Nations, New York City, on its 40th Anniversary. He was 90 years old. After the talk, Krishnamurti was given a UN Peace Medal.

We have lived on this earth for hundreds of thousands of years. During this long evolution, we have not found peace on earth. Pacem in Terris was preached long before Christianity, by the ancient Hindus and Buddhists. During all this time, we have lived in conflict with our neighbours and people of our own community, with our society and family. We have fought and struggled against each other for millennia upon millennia. Historically there have been wars practically every year, and we are still at war. The religious hierarchy has talked about peace on earth, goodwill among men, but it has never come about. They have spoken of peace when you die: going to heaven and having peace there.

One wonders, if one is at all serious, why we kill other human beings—in the name of God, in the name of peace, in the name of some ideology, or for one's country, king or queen and all the rest of that business. And religions, whether it be Christianity, Islam, Hinduism or

1

Buddhism, are also at war with each other. Nations are at war, groups are at war, ideologies, whether the Russian or the American, or any other category of ideology, are at war with each other, in conflict. After so many centuries, why is it that we cannot live peacefully on this marvellous earth? This question has been asked over and over again. This organisation, the United Nations, has been formed around that. What is the future of this organisation? After its 40th year, what lies beyond?

Time is a strange factor in life. Time is important for all of us. And the future is what is present. The future is now. The present, which contains the past, modifying itself now, becomes the future. This has been the cycle of time, the path of time. And now, at the present time, if there is no radical change, no fundamental mutation, the future is what is now. This has been proven historically, and we can prove it in our daily lives.

We are human beings, you and I, and as long as we are in perpetual conflict with each other, there will be no peace on this earth. We talk about peace endlessly. The Catholic hierarchy talks about Pacem in Terris but has been responsible for appalling wars in the past—a hundred years of war, torture; all kinds of horrible things they have done to human beings. And other religions have had their own kinds of war.

So the future beyond this 40th anniversary is what is going on now. One wonders if we realise that. The present is not only the past but also contains the future. The past modifies itself constantly through the present and projects the future. If we don't stop our quarrels, struggles, antagonism and hatred now, it will be like this tomorrow. And you can stretch out that tomorrow for a thousand years.

So it behoves us to ask ourselves whether we as human beings can live peacefully with each other. Organisations have not solved this problem. You can reorganize, but war still goes on. So organizations, whether a world organization or a particular kind of organization to bring about peace, will never succeed because human beings individually, collectively and nationally are in conflict. Stronger nations like America or Russia are at war with each other economically and ideologically. So peace cannot possibly exist on this earth if there are nationalities, which is glorified tribalism. We need security, and we invest in nationalism, or an ideology or belief. Beliefs, ideologies and so on have separated us, and organizations cannot possibly bring about peace between you and me. We believe in ideologies—you believe in God, and others don't.

I wonder if you have ever considered that religions based on a single book, such as the Koran or Bible, become very bigoted, narrow and fundamentalist. Religions like the Hindu and Buddhist have many books considered sacred and are not so bigoted; they are more tolerant. But there is ongoing conflict: those who put faith in books and those who do not, and there is the conflict between the one book and those who accept other books.

So we are asking deeply, if we are serious, whether you and I, and those of us who are involved in organizations, can live at peace with each other. Peace requires a great deal of intelligence, not just demonstrations against a particular form of war, the nuclear bomb, for example, which is a product of brains entrenched in nationalism, a belief or ideology. They also talk about peace and, at the same time, supply armaments to the rest of the world.

It is a vast, cynical world, and cynicism can never tolerate affection, care and love. We have lost the quality of compassion. Please do not analyse what we mean by compassion—one can analyse it very easily. But you cannot analyse love. Love is not within the limits of the brain because the brain is the instrument of sensation, the centre of all reaction and action, and we try to find peace and love within this limited area. This means thought is not love, because thought is based on experience and knowledge which are limited, whether now or in the future. Knowledge is always limited and is contained in the brain as memory. From that memory springs thought. This can be observed very simply and easily if one examines oneself, looks at the activity of thought, experience and knowledge. You don't have to read any book or become a specialist to understand your own ways of thinking and living.

So thought is always limited, whether it is now or in the future. And we try to solve our problems, technological, religious and personal, through the activity of thought. Thought is not love. Love is not sensation or pleasure; it is not the result of desire. It is something entirely different. To come upon that love, which is compassion, with its own intelligence, one has to understand oneself, what one is. Not through analysis, but understanding your own sorrows, pleasures and beliefs.

Wherever you go in the world, human beings suffer for various reasons. It might be petty, or a very deep incident that has caused pain and sorrow. Every human

4

being on this earth goes through this. Sorrow is shared by all human beings. It is not yours or mine, but humanity's sorrow, along with anxiety, pain, loneliness, despair and aggressiveness. So we are the rest of humanity; we are not separate human beings psychologically. You may be a woman, I may be a man, you may be tall, I may be short, but inwardly, psychologically, we are the rest of humanity. You are the rest of humanity, and so if you kill another, if you are in conflict with another, you are destroying yourself. You can observe this if you look at yourself very carefully without any distortion.

So there can only be peace when humanity, when you and I, have no conflict in ourselves. You might say, 'If one comes to the end of all conflict within oneself, how will it affect the rest of humanity?' That is an old question. Instead, we have to ask whether sorrow, pain and anxiety can ever end in ourselves. If one applies, looks, observes with great attention, as you look with considerable attention when you are combing your hair or shaving, with heightened quality of attention you can observe yourself, all the nuances and subtleties. The mirror is your relationship with other human beings. In that mirror, you can see yourself exactly as you are. But most of us are frightened to see what we are, and so we gradually develop resistance and guilt, and we never ask for total freedom.

So can we live on this earth, Pacem in Terris, with great understanding of humanity, which is to understand yourself profoundly? We can, without turning to the professionals but as simple laypeople. We can observe our idiosyncrasies and tendencies. The brain has been conditioned to war, hate and conflict through this long period of evolution. Can that brain, with its cells that contain memories, free itself from its own conditioning? It is very simple to answer such a question.

If you have been going north all the days of your life, as humanity has been going in a particular direction, which is in conflict, and somebody serious comes along and says, 'That leads nowhere. Go south, go east, any other direction but north,' when you actually move away from that direction, there is a mutation in the very brain cells themselves because you have broken the pattern. And that pattern must be broken now, not forty or a hundred years later.

1

WHAT CAN I DO?

We ought to ask fundamental questions of ourselves and not await answers from others. These fundamental questions must be answered by each of us, and we must not depend on theoreticians, however clever, erudite, scholarly or experienced. For the world is in terrible confusion, with mounting sorrow, and we are responsible for this; each human being throughout the world is responsible for this frightening confusion. Apparently, we depend on others for explanations and are satisfied with these explanations, but all explanations are verbal and therefore of no great importance. Any description, any explanation of the actual state of the world is useless, has no meaning. But most of us are satisfied by words, intellectual explanations woven beautifully or subtly. It seems to me that we must be beyond all explanations, whoever they are offered by.

What is important is to ask ourselves these fundamental questions and be utterly responsible in finding not only the answer, but in the very answering to act. Action is part of the question and its answer. In the fact of asking these fundamental questions and in discovering the answers for ourselves, that very discovery must be expressed in action. The questioning, the answering and the action are simultaneous and not separate. When they are separate, everything is broken up into departments and categories. Out of that division arise prejudices, conflicts, opinions and judgments. Whereas, if we could really ask, in the very asking we would discover the understanding of question and action; they are not separate. I hope we shall be able to ask ourselves these questions and understand them, not intellectually or verbally but with our hearts and minds. In this process of understanding, action takes place.

One of the fundamental questions consists of our relationship to reality. That reality has been expressed in different ways in the East and West. If we do not discover for ourselves what that relationship is, independently of the theoreticians, theologians and priests, we will be incapable of discovering what relationship with reality is. That reality may be named as God—and the name is of very little importance because the name, the word, the symbol, is never the actual. To be caught in symbols and words seems utterly foolish, and yet we are so caught, Christians in one way, Hindus, Muslims and others in other ways—and words and symbols have become extraordinarily significant. But the symbol, the word, is never the real thing.

So in asking the question, what our true relationship to reality is, one must be free of the word with all its associations, prejudices and conditions. If we do not find that relationship, life has very little meaning; then our confusion and misery are bound to grow, and life will become more and more intolerable, superficial and meaningless. One must be extraordinarily serious to find out if there is such a reality and our relationship to it.

We want to find out first if there is something immeasurable, beyond all reach of thought, above all measurement, a thing that cannot possibly be touched by words, that has no symbol. Is it possible, first of all—not mystically, romantically or emotionally, but actually—to discover or come upon this extraordinary state? The ancients and some throughout the world who have perhaps come upon it unknowingly have said there is something. Serious-minded people for millions of years have attempted to find that. Those who are casual or flippant have their own reward and way of life, but there is always a small minority who are earnest, who come upon this endless, measureless thing. To understand it, one must be free of all dogma, beliefs and traditional impediments that condition the mind, which are merely inventions of thought.

We are human beings, suffering, lonely, confused, in great sorrow. Whether we call ourselves capitalists, socialists or anything else, we are human beings. But apparently, the important thing for us is the label: French, German or any other. It is important to be free from all this because you need freedom, not merely verbally but actually. It is only in freedom that you can discover what is the real, not through beliefs and dogmas.

So, if one is very earnest, in the sense that one is willing to go to the very end, then there must be this freedom—freedom from all nationalities, freedom from all dogmas, rituals and beliefs. Apparently, this is one of the most difficult things to do. You find in India people who have thought a great deal about these matters, yet they remain soaked in Hindu tradition. In the West, they are immersed in the Catholic or Protestant dogmas, so they cannot possibly break through. And if one is to have a different kind of life, a life at a different dimension, one must not only be free consciously from all this, but also deep down in the very roots of one's being. Then only is one capable of really looking, seeing, because to find reality the mind must be sane, healthy, highly intelligent, which means highly sensitive.

What is important is to have a mind that has never been tortured, never been forced into a certain pattern. As one observes throughout the world, religions have maintained that to find reality you must torture yourself, you must deny everything, every sensuous pleasure, you must discipline yourself until your whole mind is shaped according to a pattern which has been established; so the mind, in the end, has lost the pliability, quickness, sensitivity and the beauty of movement. But what is necessary is a mind that is untortured, a mind that is very clear. And such a mind is not possible if it has any kind of prejudice.

You know, one of the most difficult things is to observe, to look: to look at anything without the image of that thing, to look at a cloud without the previous associations with regard to clouds, to see a flower without the image, memories and associations concerning flowers. These associations, images and memories create distance between the observer and the observed. In that distance, in the division between the seer and the thing seen, the whole conflict of humanity exists. It is necessary to see without the image so that the space between the observer and the thing observed is simply not there. When that space exists, there is conflict.

So the art of seeing is very important. If we see ourselves with the images we have built about ourselves, then there is conflict between the image and the fact. And all our life is this conflict between what is and what should be.

Please do not merely read these words, phrases and expressions, but observe as we go along, not analytically, but actually observe the process of your own mind; see how it is working, how it is looking at itself. Then you will be actually listening, not trying to translate what you read according to your prejudices and conditioning.

The world is in such a frightful state; there is such catastrophe and misery that we must live a different kind of life. There must be a fundamental revolution in our way of living. Humanity has apparently chosen war and conflict as the way of life, and there is a revolt among the young against all this. But unfortunately, such a revolt has very little meaning unless one has found for oneself the basic answers to the fundamental questions of life.

One of the primary questions is: what is this thing called reality? Can you and I, living our daily lives, not retiring into a monastery, becoming disciples of some guru, or running off to a strange academy in India, find this reality for ourselves? We must. Not through prayers, imitation or following somebody, but through becoming aware of our own conditioning, seeing it actually not theoretically, as you would see a flower or a cloud, seeing without separation.

Have you ever tried to look at anything or anyone, for example, at your wife or husband, without the image you have built through many years of relationship, of irritations, pleasures, anger, to look at each other without the image? I do not know if you have ever tried this, but if you have, you will have found how extraordinarily difficult it is to be free of images. It is these images that enter into a relationship, not human beings. You have an image about me and I have an image about you, and the relationship is between these two images with their symbols, associations and memories. There will be division as long as there is an image that engenders the whole structure of conflict.

So one must learn the art of looking, not only at the clouds and flowers, at the movement of a tree in the wind, but actually looking at ourselves as we are, not saying, 'I am ugly,' 'I am beautiful,' or 'Is that all?'—all the verbal assertions that one has with regard to oneself. When we can look at ourselves clearly, without the image, perhaps we shall be able to discover what is true for ourselves. And that truth is not in the realm of thought but of direct perception, in which there is no separation between the observer and the observed.

One of the fundamental questions is our relationship to the ultimate, the nameless, and what is beyond all words. Then there is the fundamental question of our relationship to others. This relationship is society, the society we have created through our envy, greed, hatred, brutality, competition and violence. Our chosen relationship to society, based on a life of battle, wars, conflict, violence and aggression, has gone on for thousands of years and has become our daily life, in the office, at home, in the factory, in churches.

We have invented a morality out of this conflict, but it is no morality at all; it is a morality of respectability, which has no meaning whatsoever. You go to church and love your neighbour there, and in the office you destroy them. There are nationalistic differences based on ideas, opinions, prejudices, a society in which there is terrible injustice and inequality—we all know this, we are terribly aware of all this; aware of the war that is going on, of the action of the politicians and the economists trying to bring order out of disorder. We are aware of this and we say, 'What can we do?' We are aware that we have chosen a way of life that leads ultimately to the field of murder. We have probably asked this, if we are at all serious, but we say 'I, as a human being, can't do anything. What can I do faced with this colossal machine?'

When one puts a question to oneself such as 'What can I do?' one is putting the wrong question. To that, there is no answer. If you do answer it, you will form an organization, belong to something, commit yourself to a particular course of political, economic, social action, and you are back again in the same old circle in your particular organization with its presidents, secretaries, money, your own little group against other groups. We are caught in this. 'What can I do?' is a totally wrong question—you cannot do a thing when you put the question that way. But you can, when you actually see that each one of us is responsible for the wars that are going on in the world, that you and I are responsible, actually, desperately responsible for what is going on everywhere. We are responsible for the politicians, whom we have brought into being, responsible for the army trained to kill, responsible for all our actions, conscious or unconscious.

But we say, 'I don't want to be responsible.' We are frightened to say, 'I am responsible for this whole monumental mess.' But if you actually with your heart feel this thing, you will act. Then you will find that you are totally outside society. You may have a few clothes, go about in a car and all the rest of it, but you are truly moral, psychologically, inwardly. You are completely out of society, which is to deny all morality. If you accept the present structure of morality, you are actually immoral.

There is corruption; society is going downhill. You know about the riots in America and about what is happening in the Middle East and Far East, and in India where there is immense poverty. Each country feels that it has to solve the problems for itself, while politicians throughout the world are playing a game with starvation, with murder, because we have divided the world into nationalities, into sovereign governments with different flags. And to bring about order, the concern of every human being must be the unity of humanity. That means a government that is not divided into French, German and all the other nationalities.

Don't you wonder why politicians exist at all? A government can be run by computers, impersonal, non-ambitious, not people seeking their own personal glory in the name of their nation. Then we might have a sane government! But unfortunately, human beings are not sane; we want to live in this immense mess. And you and I are responsible for it. Don't, please, merely agree; you have to do something about it. The doing is the seeing, the listening.

When you see a danger, you act. There is no hesitation, no argument, no personal opinion—there is immediate action. But you don't see the immense danger of what is going on in the world around you, in the educational system, in the business world, in the religious world—you don't see the danger of all that. To see the danger of it is to act. When you see something actually, there is no conflict;

14

there is the immediate movement away from the thing, without resistance, without conflict.

To look at social injustice, social misery, social morality and culture, in the midst of which organized religions exist, and to deny their validity psychologically, is to become extraordinarily moral. Because, after all, morality is order; virtue is complete order. And that can only come into being when you deny disorder, the disorder in which we live, the disorder of conflict and fear in which each individual is seeking personal security.

I do not know if you have ever considered the question of security. We find security in commitment. In being committed to something, there is a great feeling of security—in being French or English, or anything else. That commitment gives us a feeling of security. If you have committed yourself to a course of action, that commitment gives a great deal of surety, assurance, certainty. But that commitment always breeds disorder, and this is what is actually taking place. I am a socialist, but you are not. We are committed to ideas, to theories, to slogans, and so we divide: you are this and I am that. Whereas if we are involved, not committed, in the whole movement of life, there is no division. Then we are human beings in sorrow, not a French person in sorrow or a Catholic in sorrow, but human beings who are guilty, anxious, in agony, lonely, bored with the routine of life. If you are involved in it, we will find a way out of it together. But we like to be committed; we like to be separately secure, not only nationalistically or communally, but individually. And in this commitment is isolation. When the mind is isolated, it is not sane.

We may all know this verbally, read a great deal about it, but unfortunately what we have read does not constitute a discovery of ourselves; it is not our own discovery, our own understanding. For that, one must investigate, look at oneself without any criteria, look at oneself with choiceless awareness so as to see exactly what one is, not what one should be. And when you see exactly what you are, there is no conflict.

Also there is the question of love and death. Again, the thing we call love has really lost its meaning. When one says, 'I love you,' pleasure is abundant in this. So one has to find out for oneself if love is pleasure. This doesn't mean one must deny pleasure to find love, but when love is hedged about with greed, jealousy, hate, envy, as it is with most of us, is this love? When love is divided into the divine and ordinary, sensuous love, is it love? Or is not love something that is not touched by pleasure?

One has to go into this question of what pleasure is. Why is everything based on pleasure? The search for what you call God is based on pleasure. One derives pleasure from having possessions, from prestige, position, power, domination. But without love, do what you will, be as clever as you like, you will solve nothing. Whatever you do, you will create more misery for yourself and another.

Then we come again to this extraordinary question of the nature of death. This must be answered neither with fear, nor by escaping from that absolute fact, nor by belief, nor hope. There is an answer, the right answer, but one has to put the right question to find the right answer. But you cannot possibly put the right question if you are merely seeking a way out of it, or if the question is born of fear, despair or loneliness. If you do put the right question with regard to reality, with regard to our relationship to each other, and what that thing called love is, and this immense question of death, then out of the right question will come the right answer. From that answer comes right action. Right action is in the answer itself, and we are responsible.

Don't fool yourself by saying, 'What can I do? As an individual, living a shoddy little life, with its confusion and ignorance, what can I do?' Ignorance only exists when you don't know yourself. Self-knowing is wisdom. You may be ignorant of all the books in the world, and I hope you are, of the latest theories, but that is not ignorance. Not knowing oneself deeply, profoundly, is ignorance. You cannot know yourself if you cannot look at yourself, see yourself actually as you are, without any distortion or any wish to change. If you do, what you see is transformed because the distance between the observer and the observed is removed, and hence there is no conflict.

2

WHAT IS YOUR RESPONSIBILITY TO SOCIETY?

It must be fairly obvious to each one of us when we look at the world that there must be some kind of fundamental revolution. I am using that word to convey not a superficial, patchwork reformation, not a revolution instigated as a calculated risk according to a particular pattern of thought, but the revolution that can come about only at the highest level when we begin to understand the full significance of the mind. Without understanding this fundamental issue, any reformation, however beneficial temporarily, is bound to lead to further misery and chaos.

Seeing this extraordinarily complex pattern of wealth and poverty, of sovereign governments, of armies and the latest instruments of mass destruction, one asks oneself what will come out of all this chaos and where it will lead. What is the answer? If one is at all serious, one must have asked oneself this question. How are we,

18

as individuals and groups, to tackle this problem? Being confused, most of us turn to a pattern, religious or social; we look to a leader to guide us out of this chaos, or we insist on returning to the ancient traditions. We say, 'Let us go back to what the Upanishads said; let us have more prayers, more rituals, more gurus.'

Now, looking at this whole chaotic picture—not philosophically, not merely as an observer watching the events go by, but as one whose sympathies are stirred and who has a germ of compassion, which I am sure most of us have—how do you respond to it all? What is your responsibility to society? Or are you merely caught in the wheels of society, following the traditional pattern set by a particular culture, Western or Eastern, and are therefore blind to the whole issue? And if you do open your eyes, are you merely concerned with social reform, political action, economic adjustment? Does the solution to this enormously complex problem lie anywhere there, or does it lie in a totally different direction? Is the problem merely economic and social? Or is there chaos and the constant threat of war because most of us are not concerned with the deeper issues of life, with the total development of humanity?

Now, seeing this state of things—of which I am sure you are very much aware unless you are insensitive or are trying to block it out— what is your answer? Please do not answer theoretically, according to the socialist, the capitalist, the Hindu or some other pattern, which is merely an imposition and therefore not true. Instead, strip the mind of all its immediate reactions, the so-called educated reactions, and find out what your reaction is as an individual. How would you solve this problem?

If you ask a communist this question, they have a very definite answer, and so has the Catholic, Hindu or Muslim, but their answers are obviously conditioned. They have been educated to think along certain lines, narrow or wide, by a society or culture which is not at all concerned with the total development of the mind. Because they respond from their conditioned thinking, their answers are inevitably in contradiction and must therefore always create enmity—which is again fairly obvious. If you are a Hindu or Christian, or what you will, your response is bound to be according to your conditioned background, the culture in which you have been brought up. The problem is beyond all cultures, beyond any particular pattern, yet we are seeking an answer in terms of a pattern, and hence there is mounting confusion and greater misery. So unless there is a fundamental breaking away from all conditioning, a total cleavage, we shall create more chaos, however well-intentioned or so-called religious we may be.

It seems that the problem lies at a different level altogether. In understanding it, we shall bring about an action entirely different from the socialistic or the capitalistic pattern. The problem is to understand the ways of the mind because unless one is able to observe and understand the process of thought in oneself, there is no freedom, and hence one cannot go very far. With most of us, the mind is not free; it is consciously or unconsciously tethered to some form of knowledge, to innumerable beliefs, experiences and dogmas. How can such a mind be capable of discovery, of searching out something new?

To every challenge, there must be a new response, because today the problem is entirely different from what it was yesterday. Any problem is always new; it is undergoing transformation all the time. Each challenge demands a new response, and there can be no new response if the mind is not free. So freedom is at the beginning, not just at the end. Revolution must begin, surely, not at the social, cultural or economic level, but at the highest level. And the discovery of the highest level is the problem—the discovery of it, not the acceptance of what is said to be the highest level. One can be told what the highest level is by a guru, some clever individual, and one can repeat what one has heard, but that process is not discovery; it is merely the acceptance of authority. Most of us accept authority because we are lazy—it has all been thought out, and we merely repeat it like a gramophone record.

Now, I see the necessity of discovery because it is obvious that we have to create a totally different kind of culture—a culture not based on authority but on the discovery by each individual of what is true. And that discovery demands complete freedom. If a mind is held, however long its tether, it can only function within a fixed radius, and therefore it is not free. So what is important is to discover the highest level at which revolution can take place. That demands great clarity of thought; it demands a good mind, not a phoney mind which is repetitive, but a mind that is capable of hard thinking, of reasoning to the end, clearly, logically, sanely. One must have such a mind, and only then is it possible to go beyond.

So revolution can take place only at the highest level, which must be discovered. You can discover it only through self-knowledge, not through the knowledge gathered from ancient books or the books of modern analysts. You must discover it in relationship—discover it, and not merely repeat something you have read or heard. Then you will find that the mind becomes extraordinarily clear. After all, the mind is the only instrument we have, and if that mind is clogged, petty, fearful, as most of our minds are, its belief in God, its worship, its search for truth has no meaning at all.

It is only the mind that is capable of clear perception, and therefore of being very quiet, that can discover whether there is truth or not. It is only such a mind that can bring about revolution at the highest level. Only the religious mind is truly revolutionary. The religious mind is not the mind that repeats, that goes to church or to the temple, that does puja every morning, that follows some kind of guru or worships an idol. Such a mind is not religious; it is a silly, limited mind. Therefore it can never freely respond to challenge.

This self-knowledge is not to be learned from another. I cannot tell you what it is, but one can see how the mind operates. Not just the mind that is active every day but the totality of the mind, the mind that is conscious as well as hidden. All the many layers of the mind must be perceived, investigated—which does not mean introspection. Self-analysis does not reveal the totality of the mind because there is always the division between the analyser and the analysed. But if you can observe the operation of your own mind without any sense of judgment or evaluation, condemnation or comparison—just observe it as you would observe a star, dispassionately, quietly, without any sense of anxiety—

you will see that self-knowledge is not a matter of time, that it is not a process of delving into the unconscious to remove the motives, or to understand the various impulses and compulsions.

What creates time is comparison, and because our minds are the result of time, we are always thinking in terms of the "more", which we call progress. So, being the result of time, the mind is always thinking in terms of growth, of achievement. Can the mind free itself from the "more", which is to dissociate itself completely from society?

Society insists on the "more". After all, our culture is based on envy and acquisitiveness, is it not? Our acquisitiveness is not only of material things but also in the realm of so-called spirituality, where we want to have more virtue, to be nearer the Master, the guru. So the whole structure of our thinking is based on the "more", and when one completely understands the demand for the "more", with all its results, there is surely a complete dissociation from society. And only the individual who is completely dissociated from society can act upon society. The one who puts on a loincloth or a sannyasi's robe, who becomes a monk, is not disassociated from society; they are still part of society, only the demand for the "more" is at another level. They are still conditioned by, and therefore caught within, the limits of culture.

This is the real issue, not how to produce more things and distribute what is produced. The basic problem is that we are not creative; we have not discovered for ourselves this extraordinary source of creativity which is not an invention of the mind.

There can be fundamental revolution only when we understand our relationship to the collective

In all our relationships—with people, with nature, with ideas, with things—we seem to create more and more problems. In trying to solve one problem, whether economic, political, social, collective or individual, we introduce many other problems. We seem somehow to breed more and more conflict and need more and more reform. All reform needs further reform, and therefore it is retrogression. As long as revolution, whether of the left or right, is merely the continuation of what has been in terms of what shall be, it is retrogression. There can be a fundamental revolution, a constant inward transformation, only when we, as individuals, understand our relationship to the collective.

The revolution must begin with each one of us and not with external, environmental influences. After all, we are the collective: the conscious and unconscious in us are the residue of political, social and cultural influences. Therefore, to bring about a fundamental outward revolution, there must be a radical transformation within each one of us, a transformation that does not depend on environmental change.

It must begin with you and me. All great things start on a small scale; all great movements begin with you and me as individuals, and if we wait for collective action, such collective action, if it takes place at all, is destructive and conducive to further misery.

So, revolution must begin with you and me. That revolution, that individual transformation, can take place only when we understand relationship, which is the process of self-knowledge. Without knowing the whole process of my relationship at all its different levels, what I think and do has no value at all. What basis have I for thinking if l do not know myself? We are so desirous to act, so eager to do something, bring some kind of revolution or amelioration, some change in the world, but without knowing the process of ourselves inwardly, we have no basis for action, and what we do is bound to create more strife.

The understanding of oneself does not come through the process of withdrawal from society or through retirement into an ivory tower. If you and I go into the matter carefully and intelligently, we will see that we can understand ourselves only in relationship and not in isolation. Nobody can live in isolation. To live is to be related. It is only in the mirror of relationship that I understand myself, which means that I must be extraordinarily alert in my thoughts, feelings and actions. This is not a difficult process or a superhuman endeavour.

As with all rivers, while the source is hardly perceptible, the waters gather momentum as they move and deepen. In this mad and chaotic world, if you go into this process advisedly, with care, with patience, without condemning, you will see how it begins to gather momentum and that it is not a matter of time.

Where does one begin to bring about the fundamental change that is essential in the social order?

We realize that there must be a fundamental change in our way of thinking, a radical transformation of the human mind and heart. This extraordinary change cannot be brought about by merely continuing what has been in a modified form. Nor can this radical revolution in the mind be brought about through education as it now exists, for what we now call education is merely the learning of a technique to earn a livelihood and conforming to the pattern imposed by society.

So, seeing this, where are we to begin? Where does one begin to bring about this fundamental change which is so obviously essential in the social order? Surely, the individual problem is the world problem. Society is what we have made it.

There are those who have and those who have not, those who know and those who are ignorant, those who are fulfilling their ambition and those who are frustrated; there are the religions with their ceremonies and dogmatic beliefs, and there is the ceaseless battle within society, everlasting competition with each other to achieve, to become. All this is what you and I have created. Social reforms may be brought about through legislation or tyranny, but unless the individual radically changes, they will always overcome the new pattern to suit their psychological demands—which is again what is happening in the world.

It is very important, then, to understand the total process of individuality because only when the individual changes radically can there be a fundamental revolution in society. It is always the individual, never the group or the collective, that brings about a radical change in the world. This again is historically so.

Now, can the individual, that is, you and I, change radically? This transformation of the individual, not according to a pattern, is what we are concerned with, and it is the highest form of education. This transformation of the individual constitutes religion, not the mere acceptance of dogma or belief, which is not religion at all. The mind conditioned to a particular pattern that it calls religion, whether Hindu, Christian, Buddhist or what you will, is not a religious mind, however much it may practise all the so-called religious ideals.

The very structure of society is the structure of yourself

Because we have created this society in which we live, we are responsible for it—each one of us. It has not come into being because of some fictitious, spiritual forces. It has come about through our greed, through our ambition, through our personal likes, dislikes and enmities, through our frustrations, through our search for pleasure and satisfaction. We have created religions and dogmas out of fear. It is in this society that you live. Either you run away from society because you cannot understand it or cannot bring about a change in that society of which you are a part, or you become so engrossed in your own particular travail that you completely lose interest in the radical demand of a human mind that says that it must change.

Existence is a movement in relationship, and that existence is society. We cannot possibly go beyond the limits of our mind and heart unless we understand the structure of our own being. Society is not different from you—you are society. The very structure of society is the structure of yourself. So when you begin to understand

27

yourself, you are beginning to understand the society in which you live. It is not opposed to society.

A religious person is concerned with the discovery of a new way of life, of living in this world and bringing about a transformation in the society in which they live, because by transforming oneself, one transforms society. This is very important to understand.

What you are, the world is, and without your transformation, there can be no transformation of the world

We must realize that the world's problem is the individual's problem; it is your problem and my problem, and the world's process is not separate from the individual process. They are a joint phenomenon, and therefore what you do, what you think, what you feel, is far more important than introducing legislation or belonging to a particular party or group. That is the first truth to be realized.

A revolution in the world is essential, but a revolution according to a particular pattern of action is not a revolution. Revolution can take place only when you, the individual, understand yourself and therefore create a new process of action. We need a revolution because everything is going to pieces—social structures are disintegrating, there are wars and more wars. We are standing on the edge of a precipice, and there must be some kind of transformation, for we cannot go on as we are. The left offers a kind of revolution, and the right proposes a modification of the left, but such revolutions are not revolutions; they do not solve the problem because the human entity is much too complex to be understood through a formula. And as a constant revolution is necessary, it can only begin with you, with your understanding of yourself. That is a fact, that is the truth, and you cannot avoid it from whatever angle you approach it.

After seeing the truth of this, you must establish the intention to study the total process of yourself because what you are, the world is. If your mind is bureaucratic, you will create a bureaucratic world, a stupid world, a world of red tape; if you are greedy, envious, narrow, nationalistic, you will create a world in which there is nationalism, which destroys human beings, a social structure based on greed, division, property and so on. So what you are, the world is, and without your transformation, there can be no transformation of the world. But to study oneself demands extraordinary care, extraordinarily swift pliability, and a mind burdened with the desire for a result can never follow the swift movement of thought.

So then, the first difficulty is to see the truth that the individual is responsible, that you are responsible for the whole mess. When you see your responsibility, establish the intention to observe, and therefore bring about a radical transformation in yourself.

§

At whatever level you live, there is conflict, not only individual conflict but world conflict. The world is you; it is not separate from you. What you are, the world is. There must be a fundamental revolution in your relationship with people and ideas; there must be a fundamental change. That change must begin not outside you but in your relationships. Therefore, it is essential for a person of peace, for a person of thought, to understand oneself, for without self-knowledge one's efforts only create further confusion and misery.

Be aware of the total process of yourself. You need no guru, no book, to understand your relationship with all things from moment to moment.

§

Question: You say that, fundamentally, my mind works in the same way as everyone else's. Why does this make me responsible for the whole world?

Krishnamurti: Wherever you go throughout the world, human beings suffer, are in conflict, and they feel anxiety and uncertainty. Both psychologically and physically, there is very little security; there is fear, loneliness, despair and depression. This is the common lot of human beings whether they live in China, Japan, India, America, Russia or Europe—everybody goes through this. It is their life. And as a human being, you are the whole world, psychologically. You are not separate from the person suffering, anxious and lonely in India or America.

You are the world, and the world is you. This is a fact which very few people realize, not a philosophical concept, an idea, but a fact—as when you have a headache. And when one realizes this profoundly, the question arises: what is my responsibility? We are asking each other this question, please. It is a great shock for most people to realize that they are not individuals. We think our minds, problems and anxieties are all ours, personal. But when you see the truth of this matter, what is your responsibility? What is your responsibility globally—not only for your wife or husband and children but for the whole of humanity?

We are humanity. We have our illusions, our images of God and heaven, our rituals, exactly like the rest of the world, only with different names. The pattern is the same. What is your reaction when you feel that you are humanity? How do you respond to the challenge?

How do you meet any challenge? If you meet it from your old individual conditioning, your response will naturally be totally inadequate and fragmentary, and it will be rather shoddy. So you have to find out what your response is to this great challenge. Does your mind meet it greatly, or with your fears, anxieties and the little concerns about yourself?

The responsibility depends upon the response to the challenge. Is it just a flutter, a romantic appeal, or something profound that will transform your whole way of looking at life? Then you are no longer British, American or French. Will you give up all that or merely play with the idea, a marvellous utopian concept?

§

Question: How can the idea that you are the world and are responsible for the whole of humanity be justified on a rational, objective, sane basis?

31

Krishnamurti: One is not sure it can be rationalized on a sane, objective basis, but we will first examine it before we say it cannot.

First of all, the earth on which we live is our earth. It is not the British earth or the French, German, Russian, Indian or Chinese earth; it is our earth on which we are all living. That is a fact. But thought has divided it racially, geographically, culturally, economically. That division is causing havoc in the world. Obviously; there is no denial of that; that is rational, objective, sane. And we have been saying it is the earth of all human beings, not the earth of isolated, divided communities. It is our earth, though politically and economically we have divided it, for security reasons and various forms of patriotic, illusory reasons that eventually bring about war.

Please go into this with me. You may disagree, you may say it is all nonsense, but please listen to it and see if it is not rational, objective and sane.

We have also said that our human consciousness is similar. On whatever part of the earth we live, we all go through a great deal of suffering, a great deal of pain, great anxiety, uncertainty, fear. And we occasionally, or perhaps often, have pleasure. This is the common ground on which all human beings stand. This is an irrefutable fact. We may try to dodge it, we may try to say that we are individuals, but when you look at it objectively, non-personally, not as British or French and so on, in examining it you will find that your consciousness is like the consciousness of all human beings, psychologically. You may be tall, you may be fair, you may have brown hair, may be black or white, whatever it is, but inwardly, psychologically, we are all having a terrible time. We all have a great sense of desperate loneliness. You may have children, a husband or wife and all the rest of it, but when you are alone, you have this feeling that you have no relationship with anything, totally isolated. I am sure most of us have had that feeling. And we are saying this is the common ground on which all humanity stands. And whatever happens in the field of consciousness, we are responsible.

That is, if I am violent, I am adding violence to consciousness that is common to all of us. If l am not violent, I am not adding to it; I am bringing a totally new factor to that consciousness. So I am profoundly responsible either for contributing to violence, to confusion, to the terrible division; or as I recognize deeply in my heart, in my blood, in the depths of my being, that I am the rest of the world, I am humanity, I am the world, that the world is not separate from me, I become totally responsible. This is rational, objective, sane. The other is insanity: to call oneself a Hindu, a Buddhist, a Christian and all the rest of it. These are just labels.

So when you have that feeling, that reality, see the truth that every human being living on this earth is responsible for everything happening, how will you translate that in daily life? How will you translate it if you have that feeling? Not as an intellectual conclusion or as an ideal because then it has no reality. But if the truth is that you are standing on a ground that is common to all humanity, and you feel totally responsible, then what is your action towards society, towards the world in which you are living?

The world as it is now is full of violence. Only very, very few people escape from it. Suppose I realize I am totally responsible, what is my action then? Competitiveness between nations is destroying the world—the more

33

powerful and the less powerful, with the less powerful trying to become more powerful, and so on. Shall I, realizing that I am the rest of humanity and am totally responsible, be competitive? Please answer these questions. When I feel responsible for this, naturally I cease to be competitive.

The religious world, as well as the economic and social world, is also based on a hierarchical principle. And shall I also have this hierarchical outlook? Obviously not, because that again means there is the one who says, 'I know,' and the other who says, 'I do not know.' The one who says, 'I know,' is now taking a superior position, economically, socially, religiously, and has a status. If you want that status, go after it, but you are contributing to the confusion of the world.

So there are actual, objective, sane actions when you perceive, when you realize in your heart of hearts, in the depth of your being, that you are the rest of humanity and that we are all standing on the same ground.

> There is no way out except to become aware of this immense responsibility as a human being

As an individual, it is your responsibility to bring about a tremendous change in the world. It is your responsibility because you are part of this society, because you are part of this tremendous sorrow of humanity, this constant effort, struggle, pain and anxiety. You are responsible. Unless you realize that immense responsibility and come directly in contact with it and listen to the whole structure, the machinery of that responsibility, do what you will—go to every temple, to every guru, to every religious book in the world—your action has no meaning because those are mere escapes from actuality.

So we have to understand this existence, this life, our relationship to society. We have not only to understand our relationship with each other, with society, but bring about a radical change in that relationship. And that is our responsibility. I don't think we feel this urgency. We look to the politicians, we look to philosophy, we look to something mysterious that will bring about an alteration within ourselves.

There is no way out except that you become aware of this immense responsibility as a human being. And becoming aware of that responsibility, you learn all about it and do not bring all your previous knowledge to learn. To learn, there must be freedom, otherwise you will repeat the same thing over and over again. You cannot learn ahimsa.

There is so much confusion, misery and sorrow in the world, and we have not been able to find a way out of it. So we resort to the past. We think we must go back thousands of years and resuscitate that past to bring about a revival. And again, there is no answer that way. There is no answer through time. Time can make life happier, more comfortable, but comfort and pleasure are not the absolute answers to life. Nor does the answer lie through reform. Nor is there a way out through any temple or any sacred book. One has to realize the seriousness of all this and put away all that nonsense to come face to face with facts—which is our life, our everyday, brutal, anxious, insecure, cruel life, with its pleasures and amusements—

to see if one can bring about, as a human being who has lived for two million years, a radical transformation within oneself, and therefore within the structure of society.

To be aware of this responsibility means great, arduous work. We have to work not only within ourselves but also in our relationships with others. I mean by work, not the practising of some silly formula, absurd theory and fantastic assertions of a philosopher, guru or teacher. Those are all too infantile, immature. When we talk about work, we mean becoming aware of the responsibility, as a human being living in this world, that we have to work to bring about a change within ourselves. And if we really change, if we bring about a mutation within ourselves, we will transform society.

Society is transformed not through any economic or social revolution. We have seen this through the French Revolution and the Russian Revolution. Our everlasting hope that our inward nature can be transformed by altering outward things has never been fulfilled, and it will never be. Outward change, economic change, is not going to change our attitude, our ways of life, our misery, our confusion.

So to bring about a total change, one has to become aware of oneself—that is, learn about oneself anew. According to recent discoveries of anthropology, we have lived for two million years, and we have not found a way out of this misery. We have escaped from it, we have run away to fanciful illusions, but we have not found a way out. We have not built a totally free society; we have built a society of conformity.

There are societies that, through necessity, cooperate. Through necessity, through compulsion, through an industrial revolution, people live together; they cooperate, conform, follow a pattern. But in that society, as one can observe, there are still conflicts; people are against one another because they are ambitious and competitive, though they may talk about the love of the neighbour. By force we cooperate, but through that cooperation, through that assertion of loving the neighbour, we are competitive, ruthless, ambitious. Therefore such a pattern of society brings about its own destruction.

Then there is a form of society where there is no civic consciousness; each is out for themselves, concerned with their family, their group, their class, their particular part of the country, their linguistic division, but with no civic consciousness. We are not conscious of what is happening to our neighbour; we do not care; we are indifferent to what happens. But yet, if you observe, our religious books have told us that perhaps we will live the next life, therefore we must behave, that there is karma and what we do now will matter, how we talk, how we say things, that behaviour is righteousness and if we do not behave now, we will pay for it next life. This is the crude form. On that, we have been brought up for centuries, and yet such beliefs and ideas have no importance in our lives because we still carry on as though this is the only life that matters. Because we are competitive and ambitious, we destroy our neighbour, and so we are not at all civic-minded.

So there are these two forms of society. One form is that the human beings living in it are made to conform and cooperate out of necessity. Thus they become civic-minded: they do not throw things out on the road because they would be punished; there is order. But within that order, within that framework, each is against the other. In the other form of society, there is no framework and no civic consciousness because they do not believe in what you are being told. We have these two forms of society, and each inherently within itself, has the seed of its own destruction.

So, a religious person is concerned with creating a new society that is neither this nor that, but something entirely different: each behaves righteously every minute because they understand their responsibility as a human being.

We alone are responsible and no other—how we behave, what our activities are, whether we are ambitious, cruel, destructive, hating, jealous, competitive, what our fears are. It is only such a mind that can bring about a new society.

We do need a new society. That society is not going to be created by anybody except by you. I don't think we feel the immense responsibility of this. That is the first thing that matters because that is the foundation—righteous behaviour, right conduct. Not the conduct of a pattern but the conduct which comes about through learning. If you are all the time learning, that very learning brings about its own righteous action. Therefore it is only the religious mind that can create a new society.

THE IMPORTANCE OF THE INDIVIDUAL

Without a radical transformation of the individual, society becomes a burden, an irresponsible continuity in which the individual is merely a cog.

> If you would bring order out of this
> chaos, where would you begin?

Life is a complex problem, and to understand it there must be patient analysis of the problem and not jumping to a comforting conclusion. There must be a sane detachment to understand the actual existing problem, so let us take the journey of understanding. In making this journey, do not let us jump to any conclusion and action.

We shall act, not based upon any conclusion but upon truth. If we are attached, committed to any form of action, we shall not be capable of understanding the complex process of living. If we are too close to the problem, we are incapable of right observation and comprehension. If we are to understand life, there must be no conclusion, for conclusions put an end to right thinking. As living is a vast process, any conclusion would be petty and biased.

So let us discuss the problem of living together, if we can, seriously and earnestly, and not merely listen superficially. Though I may talk, your own life is concerned, your joys and pains, your sorrow and strife.

As every phase of life is interrelated, we must not approach it through any exclusive, specialized path. The merely intellectual or merely emotional, the psychological or the physiological, prevents understanding of the total process, which is life. In emphasizing one path, one phase, we only create conclusions that prevent understanding of the whole. If we only study or specialize in one corner of the picture, we shall not comprehend the significance of the whole. If you specialize in economics and try to comprehend life from that limited point of view, you will inevitably miss the deeper and wider significance of life and so bring about greater confusion.

For the time being, put aside your specializations and look at life as a whole. The more we specialize, the more limited and destructive we become. Our human problems are not to be solved by specialists and experts. The few that can comprehend the entire picture, the whole process of life, will be the saviours and not the specialists or the experts.

Life, living and action, is a very complex problem that must be approached very simply. If you would understand a child, a complex entity, you must not impose upon them your conditioning; you must observe without condemnation. If you see a lovely sunset and compare it with other sunsets you have seen, then the present sunset has no joy.

To understand, there must be a mind that is simple, not an innocent mind but that which perceives directly and does not translate according to its conditioning. This is one of our major difficulties in the right approach to the comprehension of life.

What is your relationship to the present degradation and chaos, to the prevailing despair? Perhaps you are not deeply aware of this degradation and despair. Everywhere, we see the utter failure of religion and education, the collapse of systems, either of the left or right. What is your relationship to this frightful confusion, to this destructive chaos? If you would bring order out of this chaos, where would you begin? Obviously, with yourself, for your relationship with this crisis, with this degradation, is direct.

Let us not blame this disaster on the few unbalanced leaders or on systems, for you have created this confusion. So to bring order and peace out of it, you must begin with yourself; you must put order in your own house. Do not let us consider the rightness or wrongness of systems and formulas which promise hope; do not let us consider theories or outer revolutions; we must begin with ourselves, for we, you and I, are responsible for this disaster and confusion.

Without you there is no world; you are the world, you are the problem. This assertion is not an intellectual formulation but an actual fact. Do not set it aside, which only indicates your desire to escape from it.

When you recognize your obvious responsibility for the strife and sorrow, what you think, feel and do, what you are, becomes vitally significant. Because you are unwilling to face it, you look to systems, to formulas, to comforting escapes. It is a fact that you are the world, and you are responsible for this aching confusion. You are the problem, and there is no independent problem apart from you. You have to understand yourself if you would bring peace and order.

When you are aware of this fact, you have to act positively and vigorously. Because you are afraid of such an action, you look to systems and leaders. The only essential starting point is you. Your individual responsibility is denied, smothered by giving importance to systems, political or religious.

Systems or formulas to save humanity become more important than ourselves. Organized society takes away individual responsibility; it makes us conform. And society, the state, becomes more important than the individual; through bureaucracy, the boredom of office and routine, the individual creative responsibility is slowly destroyed. The organized religion of dogma and belief saps away individual responsibility and freedom. Through belief and dogma, you feel secure, so you bring into being organized religion, the state, the system. You become unimportant through the efficiency of the machine, political or mechanical; industry and political parties assume great significance, and you become merely a tool to be made efficient, to be a unit of a doctrine. This is happening to you; you are responsible for this death and irresponsibility, and yet you do not realize this fact.

Instead of awakening you to creative responsibility, education is turning you out to be specialists along different lines: lawyers, police, the army and so on. You are educated, and you cease to be an individual with deep significance. The more you are educated, the more you are conditioned; the more you read, the more you repeat, the less you are capable of revolutionary thinking. Regimentation is imposed upon you through the activities of society, state, education and so on. So these and other factors make you a repetitive machine, unaware of your responsibility and significance.

To bring order and peace out of this darkness and misery, you have to start with yourself and not with the system, for psychologically you are always the master of the machine or system. You are of the greatest significance and not the society or the state, for your relationship with another is society. What you think, feel and do is of the utmost importance, for you create the environment and the state.

> It is a great mistake to say that our problems are to be solved through collective or mass action

It must be fairly obvious to most of us that a different kind of thinking and action must be brought about in the world. That requires very careful observation of ourselves, not mere analysis but deep penetration into the activities of each one of us.

The problems of our daily existence are numerous, and we have not the means or capacity to deal with them. As our lives are so drab, dull and stupid, we try to escape from them, either intellectually or mystically. Intellectually we become cynical, clever and very learned; mystically, we try to develop powers or follow some guru, hoping to make our hearts more lovely and give our lives more zest. Or, seeing the drabness of our life and the implication of our problems, and seeing that problems are always increasing, multiplying, we think that to bring about a fundamental change we cannot act as individuals but must act in a mass, collectively.

It is a great mistake to say that our problems are to be solved through collective or mass action. We believe that individual action is of very little importance and has no place when the problems are so vast, complex and demanding. Therefore we turn to collective or mass action. We think that if you and I acted individually, it would have very little result, so we join mass movements and take part in collective action. But if we examine collective action very closely, we see that it is based on you and me. We seem to regard mass action as the only effective action because it can produce a result, and we forget that individual action is much more effective because the mass is composed of many individuals. The mass is not an independent entity; it is not different or separate from you and me.

So, what is important is to understand that any creative and effective action can be brought about only by individuals, that is, by you and me. Mass action is really an invention of the politician, is it not? It is a fictitious action in which there is no independent thought and action on the part of the individual.

If you look at history, all great movements that resulted in collective action began with individuals like you and me, capable of thinking very clearly and seeing things as they are. Those individuals, through their understanding, invite others, and then there is collective action. After all, the collective is composed of individuals, and it is only the response of the individual, of you and me, that can bring about a fundamental alteration in the world. But when the individual does not see their own responsibility, they

44

throw the responsibility onto the collective, and the clever politician or religious leader then uses the collective. Whereas if you see that you and I are responsible for the alteration of the conditions in the world, then the individual becomes extraordinarily important and not merely an instrument, a tool in the hands of another.

So, you, the individual, are part of society. You are not separate from society: what you are, society is. Though society may be an entity apart from you, you have created it, and therefore you alone can change it. But instead of realizing our responsibility as individuals in the collective, we as individuals become cynical, intellectual or mystical; we avoid our responsibility towards definite action, which must be revolutionary in the fundamental sense. As long as the individual, which is you and I, does not take responsibility for the complete transformation of society, society will remain as it is.

We seem to forget that the world problem is the individual problem, that you and I create the problems of the world as individuals. The problems of war, starvation, exploitation and all the other innumerable problems that confront each one of us, are created by you and me. As long as we do not understand ourselves at every level, we will maintain the rottenness of the present society. So before you can alter society, you have to understand what your whole structure is: the manner of your thinking, the manner of your action, the ways of your relationship with people, ideas and things.

Revolution in society must begin with revolution in your own thinking and acting. Understanding yourself is of primary importance if you would bring about a radical transformation in society. The understanding of yourself

45

is self-knowledge. We have made self-knowledge into something extraordinarily difficult and remote. Religions have made self-knowledge very mystical, abstract and far away. But if you look at it more closely, you will see that self-knowledge is very simple and demands simple attention in relationship. Self-knowledge is essential if there is to be a fundamental revolution in the structure of society. If you, the individual, do not understand the ways of your own thought and activities, merely to bring about a superficial revolution in the outer structure of society is to create further confusion and misery. If you do not know yourself, if you follow another without knowing the whole process of your own thinking and feeling, you will be led to further confusion, to further disaster.

After all, life is relationship, and without relationship there is no possibility of life. There is no living in isolation because living is a process of relationship. Relationship is not with abstractions; it is your relationship to property, to people and ideas. In relationship you see yourself as you are, whatever you are, ugly or beautiful, subtle or gross. In the mirror of relationship, you see every new problem precisely, the whole structure of yourself as you are. Because you think that you cannot alter your relationship fundamentally, you try to escape, and this escape only creates more problems, confusion and disaster. But if instead of escaping you look at your life in relationship and understand the whole structure of that relationship, then there is a possibility of going beyond that which is very close. To go very far, you must begin very near, but to begin near is very difficult for most of us because we want to escape from what is, from the fact of what we are. Without understanding ourselves, we cannot go far.

We are in constant relationship. There is no existence without relationship. So relationship is the immediate, and to go beyond the immediate there must be an understanding of relationship. But we would much rather examine that which is very far away, that which we call God or truth, than bring about a fundamental revolution in our relationship. This escape to God or truth is utterly fictitious, unreal. Relationship is the only thing that we have, and without understanding that relationship we can never find out what reality or God is.

So, to bring about a complete change in the social structure, in society, the individual must cleanse their relationship. The cleansing of relationship is the beginning of one's own transformation.

Economic, social or scientific revolutions only affect the periphery, the outward boundaries of my mind. Inwardly, I am still the same

As society exists now, our relationships are organized. There is disorder because we are in conflict, not only within ourselves but with each other: as communities dividing themselves linguistically, nationally, religiously; divided as family opposed to community, community opposed to nation and so on. Inwardly, there is a tremendous urge to succeed, to compete, to conform; there is the drive of ambition, the despair and the boredom of everyday existence, and the despair of every human being on discovering oneself to be utterly, irredeemably lonely. All this, consciously or unconsciously, is the battleground of relationship. Unless we bring order in that relationship, whatever the economic, social or scientific revolution may produce, it will inevitably disintegrate because the whole structure of the human mind has not been understood, resolved and made free.

So our problem is that we are responsible for bringing about a complete psychological revolution because each human being is part of society, not separate from society.

There is no such thing as an individual. One may have a name, a separate family and all the rest of it, but psychologically one is not an individual because one is conditioned by society, beliefs, fears, dogmas—all those influences which are exercised by society, by the circumstances in which one lives. That is fairly obvious. We are conditioned by the society we live in, and the society we live in is created by us. We are responsible for that society, and we alone, as human beings, must bring about a transformation in that society.

That is the greatest responsibility of every human being—not to join social reforms; that is totally inadequate, a fancy of people according to their eccentric ideas. What we as human beings have to do—and to do this is our responsibility—is to bring about a psychological revolution so that the relationship between each other is based on order. That order can only come about through a psychological revolution, and this revolution can only come about when each one of us becomes gravely and tremendously responsible.

Most of us feel that someone else will bring about this revolution; that circumstances, God, beliefs, politicians, prayers, reading "sacred books" and so on, will somehow transform our minds. That is, we shift our responsibility to someone else, to a leader, to a social pattern, to an influence—such ways of thinking show utter irresponsibility and a great sense of indolence.

So this is your problem. I am not imposing this problem on you. You may not be aware of it—the speaker is merely trying to point it out to you. If you are not hungry, no amount of anybody else's saying that you are hungry will make you hungry. To be healthily hungry, your body must have a great deal of exercise. You have to be aware of this problem: that economic, political, scientific revolution is not the answer, that no leader, no authority, however tyrannical or beneficial, can bring about psychological order, except you yourself as a human being. Not in the world of heaven, if there is such a world, but in this world, and now.

So it is your problem. You may not want it. You may say, 'I wish somebody else would show me the way.' We are used to following people—in the past, religious teachers; now it is your particular guru, or some saint with peculiar idiosyncrasies. We are always bound to authority. A mind enslaved by authority for centuries, through tradition, through custom, through habit, such a mind is willing to follow and therefore shifts the responsibility onto somebody else. Such a mind cannot, under any circumstances, bring about psychological order. And that psychological order is imperative because we must lay the foundation in our daily lives. That is the only thing that matters. From the solid foundation, you can go very far, but if you have no foundation, or if you have laid your foundation on belief, dogma or authority, in the trust of someone else, then you are completely lost.

So we have to bring about a psychological transformation in our relationship with the society in which we live.

Therefore, there is no escape from it into the Himalayas, into becoming a monk or a nun, or taking up social service and all the rest of such juvenile business. We have to live in this world; we have to bring about a radical transformation in our relationship with each other, not in some distant future but now. And that is our greatest responsibility. Because if you cannot alter the psyche, the inward structure of your mind and heart, then you will be everlastingly in confusion, misery and despair.

So, if it is a problem to you, not imposed by me, and if you are at all alert, if you are at all taking note of what is happening in the world, you will inevitably have this problem facing you. You may run away from it and therefore become irresponsible, but if it is a problem to you, as it must be to every thoughtful, intelligent, sensitive human being, then the problem is: how is one to bring about this radical transformation in the psyche, in the psychological structure of the human mind?

As a human being, I am living in a particular society. That society is not different from me. I am part of that society. I am conditioned by that society. That society has encouraged my greed, envy, jealousy, ambition, brutality, and I have contributed my brutality and ambition to that society. I am part of it; I am part of the psychological structure of that society, which is me. Now, how am I to bring about a tremendous revolution within myself?

I see that any revolution—economic, social, scientific— only affects the periphery, the outward boundaries of my mind, and inwardly I am still the same. I may put on different clothes, acquire different forms of technological knowledge, work only a few hours a week and so on, but inwardly I am still in conflict; I am still ambitious, frustrated, under a terrific strain. Unless there is a tremendous transformation there, I cannot be orderly in living; there can be no freedom, no happiness, no escape from sorrow.

§

The social pattern is set up by humanity; it is not independent of us, though it has a life of its own. Humanity is not independent of it; they are interrelated. Change within the pattern is no change at all; it is a mere modification, a reformation. Only by breaking away from the social pattern without building another can you "help" society. As long as you belong to society, you are only helping it to deteriorate. All societies, including the most marvellously utopian, have within them the seeds of their own corruption. To change society, you must break away from it. You must cease to be what society is: acquisitive, ambitious, envious, power-seeking.

The psychological structure of society is far more important than the organizational side of society

You are responsible for the condition of the society in which we live. You are responsible, not the politicians, because you have made the politicians what they are— crooked, glorifying themselves, seeking position and prestige. This is what we are doing in daily life. We are responsible for society. The psychological structure of society is far more important than the organizational side of society. The psychological structure of society is based on greed, envy, acquisitiveness, competition, ambition, fear, this incessant demand of a human being wanting to be secure in all relationships, secure in property, secure in relationship to people, secure in relation to ideas. That is the structure of society that we have created. Society then imposes the structure psychologically on each one of us. Greed, envy, ambition and competition are all a waste of energy because in it there is always a conflict, endless conflict, as in a jealous person.

As we are responsible for the misery, poverty, wars and utter lack of peace, a religious person does not seek God. The religious person is concerned with the transformation of society, which is oneself. The religious person does not do innumerable rituals, follow traditions, live in a dead, past culture, or explain the Gita or Bible endlessly, endlessly chanting, or taking sannyasa—that is not a religious person; such a person is escaping from facts. The religious person is concerned totally and completely with the understanding of society, which is themselves. They are not separate from society.

Bringing about in oneself a complete, total mutation means complete cessation of greed, envy, ambition. Therefore one is not dependent on circumstances, though one is the result of circumstances—the food one eats, the books one reads, the films one sees, the religious dogmas, beliefs, rituals and all that business. You are responsible, and as a religious person you must understand yourself, who is the product of the society you have created. Therefore to find reality, you must begin here, not in a temple, not in an image—whether the image is graven by the hand or by the mind. Otherwise, how can you find something totally new, a new state?

4

ON POLITICS

We want to bring order within society, but how are we to do it?

Question: Since the major causes of catastrophe in the world arise from the malfunctioning social organization, is there not danger in overemphasizing the need for individuals to change themselves, even though the change is ultimately necessary?

Krishnamurti: What is society? Is it not the relationship of one individual with another? If individuals are ignorant, cruel, ambitious and so on, their society will reflect all that they are in themselves.

The questioner suggests that the conflicting relationship of individuals, which is society with its many organizations, should be changed. We all see the necessity and importance of social change. We are all familiar with the wars, starvation, ruthless pursuit of power and so on, and some earnestly desire to change these conditions. How are you going to change them? By destroying the many or few who create disharmony in the world? Who are the many or the few? You and I. Each one is involved in it because we are greedy, possessive and crave power. We want to bring order within society, but how are we to do it?

Do you seriously think only a few are responsible for this social disorganization, these wars and hatreds? How are you going to get rid of those few? If you destroy them, you use the same means they have employed, and make yourself an instrument of hatred and brutality. Hate cannot be destroyed by hate, however much you may like to hide your hate under pleasant-sounding words. Methods determine the ends. You cannot kill to have peace and order. To have peace, you must create peace within yourself and thereby in your relationship with others, which is society.

You say that more emphasis should be laid on changing the social organization. Superficial reforms can perhaps be made, but radical change or lasting peace can surely be brought about only when the individual changes. You may say that this will take a long time, but why are you concerned about time? In your eagerness, you want immediate results. You are concerned with results and not with the ways and means; thus in your haste you become a plaything of empty promises. Do you think that the present human nature, which has been the product of centuries of maltreatment, ignorance and fear, can be altered overnight? A few individuals may be able to change themselves overnight, but not a crystallized society. This does not mean a postponing, but the one who thinks clearly, directly, is not concerned with time.

Social organization may be an independent mechanism, but it has to be run by us. We have created it, and we are responsible for it. We can be independent of it only when we as individuals do not contribute to the general hate, greed and ambition.

In our desire to change the world, we meet with opposition — groups are formed for and against, which only further engender antagonism, suspicion, and competition in conversion. Agreement is almost impossible except when there is common hate or fear. All actions born of fear and hate must further increase fear and hate.

Lasting order and peace can be brought about only when the individual voluntarily and intelligently consents to think without hate, greed, ambition and so on. Only in this way can there be creative peace within you and therefore in your relationship with another, which is called society.

Our problem is not food, clothes and shelter alone

Question: How can individual regeneration alone possibly bring about, in the immediate, the collective wellbeing of the greatest number, which is the need everywhere?

Krishnamurti: We think individual regeneration is opposed to collective regeneration. Regeneration is anonymous. It is not, 'I have redeemed myself'. As long as you think of individual regeneration being opposed to the collective, there is no relationship between the two. But if you are concerned with regeneration, not of the individual but regeneration itself, you will see there is quite a different force—intelligence—at work. After all, what are we concerned with? What is the question with which we are concerned, profoundly and deeply?

One might see the necessity for united action to save humanity. We see that collective action is necessary to produce food, clothing and shelter. That requires intelligence, and intelligence is not individual, is not of this party or that party, this country or that country. If the individual seeks intelligence, it will be collective. But unfortunately, we are not seeking intelligence; we are not seeking the solution to this problem. We have theories of our problems, ways of solving them, and the ways become individual and collective. If you and I seek an intelligent way to solve the problem, we are not collective or individual. Then we are concerned with intelligence that will solve the problem.

What is collective, what is the mass? It is you in relationship with another. This is not an oversimplification. I form a society in my relationship with you: you and I create a society in our relationship. Without that relationship, there is no intelligence; there is no cooperation on your side or my side. If I seek my regeneration and you seek your regeneration, what happens? We, both of us, are pursuing opposite directions. If both of us are concerned with the intelligent solution of the whole problem because that problem is our main concern, then our concern is not how I look at it or you look at it, not my path or your path. We are not concerned with frontiers or economic bias, with vested interests and stupidity. Then you and I are not collective, are not individual. This brings about collective integration, which is anonymous.

But the questioner wants to know how to act immediately, what to do the next moment so that our needs can be solved. I am afraid there is no such answer. There is no immediate moral remedy, whatever politicians may promise. The solution is the regeneration of the individual, regeneration which is the awakening of intelligence. Intelligence is not yours or mine; it is intelligence. It is important to see this deeply—then our political and individual action, collective or otherwise, will be quite different. We shall lose our identity; we shall not identify ourselves with something—our country, our race, our group, our collective traditions, our prejudices. We shall lose all those things because the problem demands that we lose our identity. But that requires a great, comprehensive understanding of the whole problem.

Our problem is not the bread-and-butter problem alone. Our problem is not feeding, clothing and shelter alone; it is more profound. It is a psychological problem of why one identifies oneself. And it is this identification with a party, with a religion, with knowledge, that is dividing us. And that identity can be resolved only when, psychologically, the whole process of identifying, the desire and motive, is clearly understood.

So the collective or the individual problem is non-existent when you are pursuing the solution of a particular problem. If you and I are both interested in something, vitally interested in the solution of the problem, we shall not identify ourselves with something else. But unfortunately, as we are not vitally interested, we have identified ourselves, and it is the identity that is preventing us from resolving this complex and vast problem.

There must be radical change in the political field, but such a change will have no depth if I do not pursue the 'other'

Question: Can I, religiously inclined and desirous of acting wholly and integrally, express myself through politics? For it appears that a radical change is necessary in the political field.

Krishnamurti: Seeking religiously the whole, the entire, the complete, can I politically function, that is, act partially? The questioner says politics is the path for him; when he seeks and follows that path which is not the whole, he merely functions in partial, fragmentary fields. Is that not so? What is your answer? Not your cunning answer or immediate response.

Can I see the whole of life, which means, can I love? I have compassion; I feel tremendously for the whole. Can I then act only politically? Can I, seeking the whole, be a Hindu or a Brahmin? Can I, having love in my heart, identify myself with a path, with a country, with an economic or religious system?

Suppose I want to improve the particular, bring about a radical change in the country in which I live. The moment I identify myself with that particular, have I not shut out the whole? This is your problem, just as mine; we are thinking about it together. You are not listening to me. When we are trying to find an answer, your opinions and ideas are not the solution. We are trying to find out: can a truly religious person, not a phoney one that consults others, but a really sacred person seeking the whole, can they identify themselves with a radical movement for a particular country? And will it do to have a revolution of one country, of one people, of one state, if l am seeking the whole, if I am trying to understand that which is not within the scope of the mind? Can I, using my mind, act politically?

I see there must be political action. I see there must be real change, radical change in our relationship, our economic system, the distribution of land, and so on. I see there must be revolution, and yet at the same time I am pursuing a path, the political path. I am also trying to understand the whole. What is my action there? Can you act politically, that is, partially, and understand the whole? Politics and economics are partial; they are not the whole, integrated life; they are partial, necessary, essential. Can I abandon the whole, leave the whole of society, and tinker with the particular? I cannot. But I can act upon it, not through it.

We want to bring about a certain change; we have ideas about it; we pursue so many groups, and so on. We use means to achieve the result. And is the understanding of the whole contrary to that? Am I confusing you? I am not telling you what I think; do not accept it but think it out for yourself and see. For me, political and economic action are of secondary importance, though they are essential. There must be radical change in the political field, but such a change will have no depth if I do not pursue the other. If the other is not primary, if the other is only secondary, then my action towards the secondary will have limited significance.

If I see a certain path and act politically, this political action becomes important to me, not acting integrally. But if acting integrally is really important to me and if I pursue it, political action, religious action, economic action will come rightly, deeply, fundamentally. If I do not pursue the other but merely confine myself to political, economic or social change, I create more misery.

So it all depends on what you emphasize. Laying emphasis on the right thing—which is the whole—will produce its own action with regard to politics and so on. It all depends on you. In pursuing that whole thing, without saying, 'I am going to act politically or socially,' you will bring about fundamental alterations politically, religiously and economically.

Why do specialists take charge of our lives?

Question: One sees chaos in the world is rapidly increasing. Billions are being spent on arms, and social justice is being eroded. Governments, totalitarian and democratic, are increasingly aggressive and violent. Though one sees the necessity of much deeper, fundamental human change, could you comment on the issue of active political involvement?

Krishnamurti: Am I Democratic or Republican—is that the question?

Apart from joking, why, if one may ask, do we have such great confidence in political leaders? This is the same issue in all countries. We put such confidence in the economists, in the politicians, in the leaders. Why do we do this? And what do we mean by political action?

Please, we are inquiring together; you are not just waiting for an explanation. We are thinking together over this problem, which is really a very serious problem affecting the whole of humanity.

A political group comes into power, Conservative or Labour, Republican or Democrat; they seem to have such extraordinary power, position and authority, and we follow them. They tell us what to do, and we accept them. Why is there that sense of trust in them and acceptance of their judgments?

We are sent to war by rulers, by government officials, and thousands are being killed. A majority voted them into power, and they set position and direction, and we merely follow them like sheep. Generally, they appeal to our lowest instincts, to our national pride, honour and all that business. We are stimulated by that and are willing to kill others for it, for a piece of land, and so on. Why? Why do we trust them? Please answer this question.

And what do we mean by political action different from all other actions? Why do we separate politics from daily living?

Why do we separate political activity of the left, right, centre, or extreme left, extreme right? Why, if one may ask, is political action so very different from our action of relationship, action with regard to fear in ourselves, and so on? Or is politics part of our life, not something separate? According to the common usage in the dictionary, politics is the art of government, the science of government. Why do we give this art to the politician? Apparently, they are a separate breed, different from us. Why do we depend on a politician, a guru, a priest, on anybody to govern us? Please answer this question. Why do specialists take charge of our lives? Is it that we have no so-called confidence in ourselves? Are we not sure of ourselves and so attribute clarity to politicians, to others? Is it that in ourselves we are insufficient and somebody out there is going to make us sufficient?

Are we to treat life as separate factors—political, religious, economic, and so on—or are we to treat life as a whole? Please question this. The questioner asks what political action one can take. Is that political action different from religious action, from the action of an idealist? Or does one treat life as the whole of living: learning, relationship, fears, faith, anxiety, and political action? Isn't that a whole way of living?

Are we fragmented in ourselves, into religious action, political action, family action, individual action and collective action? Can we treat life as a total movement in which all these activities are included? If we separate one from the other, we inevitably bring about contradiction. A religious life is incompatible with political life; a religious person will have no part in politics because generally politics is such a crooked affair, controlled by big industrialists, by wanting a great deal of money for the party, by dependency on rich people, and so on.

So how do we, each one of us, answer this question? There is an increase of armaments. Right now they are destroying each other, killing for God knows what. And both the democratic and totalitarian worlds are becoming more and more aggressive. How do you deal with this question? It is very easy to ask questions and find an answer from another. But if we have to answer this question ourselves, taking what is actually going on in the world, the national, religious, economic divisions, wars, tremendous spending on armaments, then what is your answer? If you are American, you say your way is the best way. Would you consider the right answer, the true answer is that we cannot separate these activities but must treat life as a whole movement?

What is political action? Would you like to start a new party, look for a new leader for the next election? You condemn the present leader, and when a new leader comes into being, there is soon doubt about them too. You know the whole thing: when the honeymoon is over, the problem begins. So what is your answer? Please go into it for yourselves. What is your answer when you have thought it out deeply? Do you ask if there is an action that is not divisible, an action that includes politics, religion, economics, everything, the whole of life? And is that possible?

> We are concerned not with reformation
> or modified continuity but with
> the fundamental transformation of
> humanity in our relationships

One sees corruption right through the world: black markets, rich people getting tremendously richer, the privileged classes and so on. Where do you begin to bring about an action that will include all actions? Where do you begin? To go very far, one must begin very near. So what is very near? Me. I am the nearest person, so I begin, but not as a selfish activity or self-centred movement. I am the nearest; I am the centre from which I start, not out there. Can I live a life that is absolutely not broken up? Not a religious life separate from all other lives and activities but a life that is political and religious. Can I live that way?

That implies, doesn't it, that I understand the whole separative activity completely and comprehend that the separate activities are contradictory, conflicting, causing endless divisions. If I understand that very clearly, perceive it not as an abstraction or as an ideal but as an actual fact, then from that observation there will be an action that will be complete.

If you want to start a political action, a new party, a new group, a new leader of your own, then I am afraid you and I won't meet; we are back into the same old pattern. We are saying that from the quality of a mind and heart of a life that is complete and sufficient psychologically, all action is included.

§

Question: Why don't you participate in politics or social reform?

Krishnamurti: Have you noticed how politics and social reform have become extraordinarily predominant in our lives? Our media is full of politics, economics and other problems. Have you ever asked yourself why it is that way, why human beings are giving such extraordinary importance to politics, economics and social reform?

Reform is necessary because of the economic, social and political confusion, and the general deterioration of the state of humanity since the World Wars. So crowds gather around political leaders; people line the streets to watch the strange animals. They try to solve the problem on the economic, social or political level, independent of the total process of humanity. Are these problems to be tackled separately, unrelated to our whole psychological problem?

You may have a perfect system that you think will solve the world's economic problems, but another will also have a perfect system. The two systems, representing two ideologies, will fight each other. As long as you are fighting over ideas and systems, there cannot be a true, radical revolution; there cannot be fundamental social transformation. Ideas do not transform people. What brings about transformation is freedom from ideas. Revolution based on ideas is no longer revolution but merely a continuation of the past in a modified state. Obviously, that is not revolution.

The questioner wants to know why I don't take part in politics or social reform. Surely, if you can understand the total process of humanity, you are dealing with the fundamental issues, not merely trimming branches of the tree. But most of us are not interested in the entire problem; we are concerned merely with reconciliation, superficial adjustment, not with the fundamental understanding of humanity as a total process. It is much easier to be an expert on one particular level. The experts on the economic or political level leave the psychological level to other experts, and we become slaves to them. We are sacrificed by experts for an idea.

So there can be fundamental revolution only in understanding the total process of yourself, not as an individual opposed to the mass, to society, but as an individual interrelated with society. Without you, there is no society. Without you, there is no relationship with another. There is no revolution, no fundamental transformation as long as we do not understand ourselves.

Reformers and so-called revolutionaries are factors of retrogression in society. A reformer tries to patch up the present society or create a new one based on an ideology, and their idea is the conditioned response to a pattern. Such a revolution, based on ideology, can never produce a fundamental, radical transformation in social relationships. We are concerned not with reformation or modified continuity, which you call revolution, but the fundamental transformation of humanity in our relationships. As long as that basic change does not take place in the individual, we cannot produce a new social order.

That fundamental transformation does not depend on belief, on religious organizations or on any political or economic system. It depends on your understanding of yourself in relationship with another. That is the real revolution that must take place. Then you as an individual will have an extraordinary influence on society. But without that transformation, merely talking about revolution or sacrificing yourself for an idea—which is not really sacrifice at all—is mere repetition, which is retrogression.

To act collectively, we must begin individually

Question: Why don't you face the economic and social evils instead of escaping into some dark, mystical affair?

Krishnamurti: I have been pointing out that only by giving importance to primary things can secondary issues be understood and solved. Economic and social evils are not to be adjusted without understanding what causes them. To understand them and so bring about a fundamental change, we have first to comprehend ourselves who are the cause of these evils.

We have, individually and so as a group, created social and economic strife and confusion. We alone are responsible for them, and thus we, individually and perhaps collectively, can bring order and clarity. To act collectively, we must begin individually. To act as a group, each one must understand and radically change the causes within oneself that produce the outer conflict and misery. Through legislation, you may gain certain beneficial results, but without altering the inner, fundamental causes of conflict and antagonism, they will be overturned and confusion will arise again. Outer reforms will ever need further reform, and this way leads to oppression and violence. Lasting outer order and creative peace can only come about if each brings order and peace within themselves.

§

Question: Why do you waste your time preaching instead of helping the world in a practical way?

Krishnamurti: Now, what do you mean by practical? You mean bringing about a change in the world, a better economic adjustment, a better distribution of wealth, a better relationship, or, to put it more brutally, helping you to find a better job? You want to see a change in the world—every intelligent person does—and you want a method to bring about that change, and therefore you ask me why I waste my time preaching instead of doing something about it.

Now, is what I am doing a waste of time? It would be a waste of time if I introduced a new set of ideas to replace the old ideology, the old pattern. Perhaps that is what you want me to do. But instead of pointing out a so-called practical way to act, to live, to get a better job, to create a better world, is it not important to find out what impediments actually prevent a real revolution? Not a revolution of the left or the right but a fundamental, radical revolution, not based on ideas. Because, as we have discussed, ideals, beliefs, ideologies and dogmas prevent action. There cannot be a world transformation, a revolution, as long as action is based on ideas because action then is merely reaction; therefore ideas become much more important than action. That is precisely what is taking place in the world.

To act, we must discover the impediments that prevent action. But most of us don't want to act, and that is our difficulty. We prefer to discuss, we prefer to substitute one ideology for another, and so we escape from action through ideology.

The world at present is facing many problems: overpopulation, starvation, division of people into nationalities and classes, and so on. Why isn't there a group of people sitting together trying to solve the problems of nationalism? But if we try to become international while clinging to our nationality, we create another problem—which most of us do. So you see that ideals are really preventing action.

Eminent authorities have said that the world can be organized and all the people fed. Then why is it not done? Because of conflicting ideas, beliefs and nationalism. Therefore, ideas are actually preventing the feeding of people. Most of us play with ideas and think we are tremendous revolutionaries, hypnotizing ourselves with such words as practical. What is important is to free ourselves from ideas, from nationalism, from all religious beliefs and dogmas, so that we can act, not according to a pattern or an ideology, but as needs demand. To point out the hindrances and impediments that prevent such action is not a waste of time; it is not a lot of hot air.

What you are doing is nonsense. Your ideas and beliefs, political, economic and religious panaceas, actually divide people and lead to war. It is only when the mind is free of ideas and beliefs that it can act rightly. One who is patriotic and nationalistic can never know what it is to be brotherly, though they may talk about it. On the contrary, their actions, economically and in every direction, are conducive to war. So there can be right action and therefore radical, lasting transformation, only when the mind is free of ideas, not superficially, but fundamentally. And freedom from ideas can take place only through self-awareness and self-knowledge.

> One who is eager to reform the world
> must first understand themselves,
> for they are the world

If the reformer, the contributor to the solution of the world's problems, has not radically transformed themselves, if they have had no inner revolution of values, then what they contribute will only add further to conflict and misery. One who is eager to reform the world must first understand themselves, for they are the world. The present misery and degradation of humanity is brought on by ourselves, and if we merely plan to reform the pattern of conflict without fundamentally understanding ourselves, we will only increase ignorance and sorrow.

To be alone is to be in a state of revolution against the whole set-up of society

The problem is this: a mind that is not innocent can never receive that which is innocent. God, truth or whatever the thing that is not nameable—the immeasurable—cannot be without an innocent mind, without a mind that is dead to all the things of society, dead to power, position and prestige, dead to knowledge. After all, power, position and prestige is what we call living. For us, that is life; for us, that is action. You have to die to that action, and you cannot do it because that is what you want. To die to the things we call living is the very living. If you go down the street and see those flags, which are the measures of power, and if you die to all that, it means you die to your own demand for power which has created this horror.

Is the way you live now really living? We want to gain heaven without going through anything; we want to be mediocre human beings, completely comfortable and secure, have our drinks and sex and power, and also have that thing we call heaven.

To be alone, which is not a philosophy of loneliness, is to be in a state of revolution against the whole setup of society—not only this society but the communist society, the fascist, every form of society as organized brutality and power. And that means an extraordinary perception of the effects of power.

Have you noticed those soldiers rehearsing? They are not human beings anymore; they are machines. They are your sons and daughters. This is happening everywhere—not only at the governmental level but also at the monastic level, belonging to monasteries, to orders, to groups who employ this astonishing power.

Aloneness is not something to be cultivated. When you see all this, you are out, and no governor or president is going to invite you to dinner. Out of that aloneness, there is humility. It is this aloneness that knows love—not power. The ambitious person, religious or ordinary, will never know what love is. If one sees all this, one has this quality of total living and therefore total action. This comes through self- knowledge.

5

ON WAR

War is the spectacular and bloody
projection of our everyday life

*Question: All except a few do not want war, so why do
they prepare for it?*

Krishnamurti: War means destruction, killing and
maiming one another, with the noise, the brutality, the
ugliness, the appalling misery of pain.

Do you know how war has come into being? It has
come because, in our daily lives, we destroy one another.
Though in the temple we talk about the love of God,
in our business dealings we cut one another's throats.
Also, we have wars because we have armies, and it is the
purpose of an army to prepare for war. Do you mean to
say that someone in an army would want to give up their
position, job and money in order to have peace? Most
would not be so stupid. So all of us, in one way or the
other, are preparing for war.

You can prevent war only if, in your daily life, you realize
that you are no longer a Hindu, Christian, Buddhist,
Muslim. If you are kind, generous, affectionate, loving

in your daily life, you will have a different world. Then, instead of squandering money on armaments, you can make this world into a paradise. But it is up to you. You have the government you deserve because you are part of that government. You are politicians in your daily lives: you want position, power and authority.

As you are responsible for war, you must be responsible for peace

As long as we use technological knowledge for the advancement and glorification of the individual or of the group, the needs of humanity can never be sanely and effectively organized. It is this desire for psychological security through technological advancement that is destroying the physical security of humanity.

There is sufficient scientific knowledge to feed, clothe and shelter us all, but the proper use of this knowledge is denied as long as there are separative nationalities with their sovereign governments and frontiers—which in turn give rise to class and racial strife. So, you are responsible for the continuance of this conflict. As long as you, the individual, are nationalistic and patriotic, as long as you hold to political and social ideologies, you are responsible for war because your relationship with another can only breed confusion and antagonism.

Seeing the false as the false is the beginning of wisdom, and it is this truth alone that can bring happiness to you and so to the world. As you are responsible for war, you must be responsible for peace. Those who creatively feel this responsibility must first free themselves psychologically from the causes of war and not merely

73

plunge into organizing political peace groups—which will only breed further division and opposition.

Peace is not an idea opposed to war. Peace is a way of life, for there can be peace only when everyday living is understood. Only this way of life can effectively meet the challenge of war, class, and ever-increasing technological advancement. This way of life is not the way of the intellect. The worship of the intellect in opposition to life has led us all to our present frustration with its innumerable escapes. These escapes have become far more important than the understanding of the problem itself. The present crisis has come into being because of the worship of the intellect. It is the intellect that has divided life into a series of opposing and contradictory actions. It is the intellect that has denied the unifying factor, which is love. The intellect has filled the empty heart with the things of the mind, and it is only when the mind is aware of its own reasoning and is able to go beyond itself that there can be the enrichment of the heart.

§

To have peace, you must live peacefully; that is, no ambition, no competition, no nationality, no class division, no petty division of race or country—linguistic or non-linguistic. To live peacefully, you must be at peace with yourself. And if you cannot be at peace with yourself, it is no good to pray for peace because everything you are doing is bringing about disorder and conflict.

A people only survive when they can meet a challenge anew; otherwise, they are destroyed

Is this vast problem of the world your problem and my problem, or is it independent of us? Is war independent of you? Is the national strife independent of you, the communal strife independent of you? The corruption, the degradation, the moral disintegration, are they independent of each one of us? This disintegration is directly related to us, and therefore the responsibility rests with each one of us. Surely, that is the main problem. To put it differently, is the problem to be left to the few leaders, either of the left or the right, to the party, a discipline, an ideology, to the United Nations, the expert, the specialist? Or is it a problem that directly involves us? This means, are we directly responsible for these problems, or are we not?

Many of you may not have thought about this; therefore it may be quite strange to you. But the question is whether the individual problem is the world problem and whether you can do anything about it.

There is the religious collapse, the moral collapse, the political corruption, the so-called independence that has produced nothing but decay. Is it your problem, or do you leave it all to chance or wait for some miracle to happen so that it will produce a revolution? Or do you leave it to an authority, to a political party?

What is your response? Don't you have to solve it, don't you have to attack it, don't you have to respond vitally to a challenge of this kind? I am not being rhetorical but merely factual. This is no place for rhetoric; that would be absurd. There is a challenge given to us all the time.

Life is a challenge, and do we respond? According to what conditioning do we respond? And when we do respond, is that response capable of meeting the challenge?

So, to meet this world catastrophe, world crisis, and enormous, unprecedented challenge, have we not to discover how we respond individually? Because, after all, a society is a relationship between you and me and another. No society is not founded on relationship. What you and I and another are, the society is. And have we not to understand that relationship between you and me and another to transform society and bring about a revolution—a complete, radical transformation? Because that is what is needed—a revolution, not of the bloody kind, not based on ideas, but a revolution of fundamental value. Not according to any pattern or ideology but a revolution born out of the understanding of the relationship between you and me and another, which is society.

So to bring about a fundamental, radical transformation in society, is it not our responsibility, our individual responsibility, to discover our direct response to this challenge? Do we respond as a Hindu, Muslim, Christian, capitalist, socialist? Is such a response a valid response, a response that will bring about a fundamental change?

If you respond to this world crisis, which is a new challenge, as a Hindu, surely you do not understand the challenge. You are merely responding to the challenge, which is new, according to an old pattern, and therefore your response has no corresponding validity or freshness. If you respond as a Catholic or a Protestant, again you are responding according to patterned thought and so your response has no significance. And has not the Hindu, the Muslim, the Buddhist, the Christian, created this problem? As the new religion is the worship of the state, the old religion was the worship of an idea.

So if you respond to a challenge according to old conditioning, your response will not enable you to understand the new challenge. Therefore, what one has to do to meet the challenge is to strip oneself completely, denude oneself entirely of the background and meet the challenge anew. Surely, a state, a country, a civilization and a people endures, lasts, only survives when it can meet a challenge anew; otherwise it succumbs and is destroyed. And that is exactly what is happening. Technologically we are tremendously advanced, but morally, spiritually, we are very far behind. With this lack of moral stamina, we meet this extraordinary technological progress, and therefore there is always friction and contradiction.

So our problem is that there is this new challenge, and all leaders have failed—spiritual, moral, political. Leaders will always fail because we choose leaders out of our confusion, so any leader will inevitably lead us to more confusion. See the importance of it; don't brush it aside as a clever statement. See the danger of a leader, not only politically but religiously. Because I am confused, I do not know what to do or how to act, and I come to you. Because I am confused, I choose you. If I am clear, I will not choose you; I do not want a leader. I am a light unto myself, and I can think out my problems for myself. It is when I am confused that I go to another. I may call them a guru, a mahatma, a political leader, and so on, but I go to them because of my confusion. I only see through the darkness of my own confusion.

One who earnestly wishes to investigate the whole catastrophic problem of sorrow must begin with themselves. It is only through the creative understanding of oneself that there can be a creative world, a happy world, a world in which ideas do not exist.

What is civilization?
It is an expression of the collective will

Question: Are individuals impotent against the atomic and hydrogen bombs?

Krishnamurti: They are experimenting with these bombs in America, Russia and elsewhere, and what can you and I do about it? What is the point of discussing this matter? You may try to create public opinion by writing to the media about how terrible it is, but will that stop governments from investigating and developing bombs? Are they not going to go on with it anyhow? They may use atomic energy for peaceful as well as destructive purposes, and probably they will have factories running on atomic energy. But they will also be preparing for war. They may limit the use of atomic weapons, but the momentum of war is there. So what can we do?

Historical events are in movement, and I don't think you and I can stop that movement. Who is going to care? But what we can do is something completely different. We can step out of the present machinery of society that is constantly preparing for war, and perhaps by our own total inward revolution, we shall be able to contribute to the building of a civilization that is altogether new.

After all, what is civilization? It is an expression of the collective will, is it not? The will of the many has created this present civilization, and cannot you and I break away from it and think entirely differently about these matters? Is it not the responsibility of serious people to do this? Must there not be serious people who see this process of destruction going on in the world, who investigate it and step out of it? What else can we do? But you see, we are not willing to be serious, and that is the difficulty. We don't want to tackle ourselves; we want to discuss something outside, far away.

This problem can only be resolved when you find out why you are angry and violent

Question: Will there be an end to these evil wars and violence?

Krishnamurti: A little boy asks because he is concerned with the future, with a world becoming more and more violent, with wars and more wars. He says, 'The older generation is creating my future, and they have produced these monstrous wars,' and he asks. 'Will there be an end to it?'

There will be an end only if you are non-violent. You must begin as an individual—you cannot make the whole world non-violent in a flash. Forget the world; be, as an individual, non-violent.

The older generation has produced this world of violence, greed and hatred; they are entirely responsible for it, not God. They have lived a life of brutality, self-concern, callousness. They have made this world, and the younger people say, 'You have made a filthy world, an ugly world,' and they are in revolt. And I am afraid their revolt will produce another form of violence, which is actually what is going on.

So, this problem of violence and wars in the future can only be resolved when you as an individual find out why you are angry, why you are violent, why you have prejudice, why you hate, and put them all away. You cannot put them away by revolting against them, but only by understanding them. Understanding them means to look, to observe, to listen. When older people talk about all the ugly things they have made, listen closely and give your attention, which means give your heart and mind to this.

You know, in the past five thousand years, there have been about fifteen thousand wars, which means three wars every year. Though we have talked about love—love of God, love of my neighbour, love of my wife or husband— talked endlessly about love, we have no love in our hearts. If we had love in our hearts, there would be a different kind of education, a different kind of business, a different world.

A nation is the glorification of the self

Question: Don't you think there are peace-loving nations and aggressive nations?

Krishnamurti: No. The term nation is separative, exclusive, and so the cause of contention and wars. There is no peace-loving nation; all are aggressive, dominant, tyrannical. As long as it remains a separate unit apart from others, taking pride in segregation, patriotism and race, it breeds untold misery for itself and others. You may not have peace and yet be exclusive. You may not have economic, social, national and racial frontiers without inviting enmity, jealousy, fear and suspicion. You may not have plenty while others starve, without inviting violence.

We are not separate; we are human beings in common relationship. your sorrow is the sorrow of another, and so by killing another you are destroying yourself. By hating another, you suffer, for you are the other. Goodwill and brotherliness are not achieved through separate and exclusive nationalities and frontiers; they must be set aside to bring peace and hope for humanity.

Why do you identify yourself with any nation, group or ideology? Is it not to protect your small self, to feed your petty and death-dealing vanities, to sustain your own glory? What pride is there in the self which brings wars and misery, conflict and confusion? A nation is the glorification of the self and so the breeder of strife and sorrow.

The unity of humanity is what matters, not one country against another

We know that war is the process of history. And we are back again. The movement of hate and war will go on unless we see that hate cannot possibly end through hate or defence. That is what we mean when we say that there must be a total revolution in the mind, so that we are no longer Christians, Buddhists, Americans, Hindus, Germans or Italians. We are human beings. The unity of humanity is what matters, not one country against another country.

To have peace, the mind must be totally unconditioned

Your own mind is conditioned, and it is this conditioning that is preventing peace, that is creating war, destruction and misery. Unless you resolve your conditioning completely, there will be no real peace in the world; there will be the peace of politicians between immense powers, which is terror.

To have peace, the mind must be totally unconditioned. One must realize that, but not superficially, not as insurance for your security or for your bank account. Peace is a state of mind; it is not the development of monstrous means of destroying each other and then maintaining peace through terror. To have real peace in the world is to live happily, creatively, without any sense of fear, without being secure in any thought, in any particular way of life. To have such peace, surely the mind must be totally free from all conditioning, either externally imposed or inwardly cultivated.

A single stone may alter the course of a river

The prevention of ever-increasing destruction and horror depends on each one of us. Not on any organization or planning, not on any ideology, not on the inventions of greater instruments of destruction, not on any leader, but on each one of us. Do not think that wars cannot be stopped by so humble and lowly a beginning. A single stone may alter the course of a river.

To go far you must begin near. To understand the world's chaos and misery, you must comprehend your own confusion and sorrow, for out of these come the magnified issues of the world. To understand yourself there must be constant meditative awareness which will bring to the surface the causes of violence and hate, greed and ambition. By studying them without identification, thought will transcend them.

None can lead you to peace save yourself; there is no leader, no system that can bring war, exploitation and oppression to an end. Only by your thoughtfulness, by your compassion, by your awakened understanding can there be established goodwill and peace.

6

OUR RELATIONSHIP TO NATURE AND THE ENVIRONMENT

If we are insensitive to nature, we must be insensitive to so many things in life

Do you notice nature, the beauty of the sky, the light of the evening stars on the sea, the palm trees, the roar of the restless sea, the song of birds in the morning, the song of a flute? Are you aware of things about us—the beauty of a smile, the fear? If we are not, is it because we are so occupied with our own travails, sorrows and problems that we have no time to see the flight of a bird? Because we do not notice nature, which is the trees, the stars, the earth, the tender leaf, we are not aware of its beauty and intensity, and so we misuse it. When we are not aware of things, we are rough with them.

It is a very odd fact that few religious paintings have nature as their theme. I don't know if you have noticed this. It is only the Chinese, I believe, that have a sense of nature in their religious pictures; here, we disregard nature. Walking down a street or in a garden, you casually break a flower. Haven't you noticed yourself doing that without thought, just pulling or treading on a flower without looking?

To us, nature means very little, and I think it is significant why it has become of so little importance in our lives. A tree, solitary against the sky, means very little to most of us. We might paint it, describe it or talk about it, but inwardly it means very little. If we don't know how to treat nature, we will not know how to treat human beings. This is essential to understand—as important to understand as the economic problems.

So why is it that nature plays such a little part in our lives? A cloud and the sunset, natural phenomena and beauty— why do these things have such little importance? Surely it is an indication of something. Should we not investigate it? Why does nature mean so little to the farmer who has to cultivate, sweat, give blood to produce? To them, it means very little, and the city dweller is indifferent to nature. Why is it that nature and its extraordinary vitality and beauty play so little a part in our lives? In understanding it, we will discover something related to our problems of food, clothing and shelter.

To appreciate something, there must be sensitivity, a quickening perception of things, but apparently we are not sensitive to nature. Do you ever see the sea, though you live near it? Apparently, we have not noticed it; I see the sea, but my mind is preoccupied with the stock market or I am too busily occupied with talk. Why is it we are insensitive? If we are insensitive with regard to nature, we must be insensitive with regard to so many things in life. We are extraordinarily insensitive in our relationship with human beings. Where there is gratification in relationship, the search for security, there cannot be sensitivity. And it is only a sensitive person who is considerate. An insensitive person can never know love.

Similarly, a mind is made insensitive by belief, ideals and the pursuit of the fictitious. And how can a mind that is dull, weary, worn out, exhausted, understand anything? So, if we are dull to nature, to the ripening corn, to the movement of a tree, to the way a person walks, if we are insensitive to all these things, how can we solve the problem of life?

Since we have lost sensitivity to nature, we are misusing nature. Someone who really loves the earth would have no war. War is exhausting; it depletes the richness of the earth. We are using soil as a means of profit. We do not love it or feel the earth, therefore directly there is insensitivity to nature. If you don't care for things, you will destroy them. The lack of love and sensitivity to the things of the earth must inevitably produce depletion and exhaustion, which is what is happening in the world, and inevitably there will be another war.

So that is one of our problems, our utter hardness with regard to nature. We have lost all sense of frugality—we want to renew our cars every year because it is the latest model. Modern production is based on this idea: make it as quickly and as weak as possible, destroy it and make new things. We keep on producing, therefore exhausting the things of the earth, and that is the way to make money. In America, they have invented a bulb that will last indefinitely, but they will not put it on the market because that won't make you buy more bulbs. The same thing with regard to cars. Engines that can be made to endure for a long time have been invented, but they will not put them on the market because they want quick turnover. That means more use of the earth and its minerals. When there is no love of the earth, you are destroying it and therefore destroying oneself.

§

What is human nature? Is it the product of environment, or is there such thing as human nature apart from environment? Some schools of thought maintain that there cannot be any distinction between human nature and environment; by altering the environment, human nature can be moulded to anything one wishes. After all, greed is merely the result of a false environment. There may be a few who are unhealthily neurotic, even though they have the right environment, who produce greed, but I am not answering to that particular twisted mind. If society were organized truly, and if every individual tried to understand the environment, the surrounding conditions in which they live, intelligence will do away with greed. Then greed is not a vice to be fought against; it is not a sin.

There cannot be a perfect environment and therefore perfect human nature, but where there is intelligence it can master environment, and therefore we can be free of reactions to that environment. The environment or society urges you to be self-protective because our whole economic and spiritual system is based upon that. But if you begin to understand the environment which produces greed, then in seeing the significance of environment, you break down greed altogether and you do not replace it with its opposite.

As you are the product of the
environment, when you change,
you affect the world.

Relationship between people, as we know it now, is a process of isolation. Though we say we are related to each other, we are merely looking over the walls of isolation— and that we call relationship. There can be relationship, true relationship, only when these walls of isolation are broken. Because human beings in their relationship to nature are so rough, crude, brutal, they are destroying not only the things of the earth but themselves. In our greed, in our self-expansive process, in our drive for power, position and authority, we are devastating the earth.

We seem to think individual revolution is of little significance.

We are concerned with the alteration or modification of the social structure, of the masses. We talk about how to affect the masses, how to bring about this experience or that knowledge, a reform in the social structure. We are more concerned with society than with the revolution of the individual. This is the same cry throughout the world, that somehow the masses must be transformed— somehow this inchoate thing must be informed, instructed, transformed or changed.

So it is important to discuss these two points and see the truth of them, whether the mass, as we call it, actually exists or is only theoretical, and how the individual revolution, the transformation of the individual, the "you" and the "me", does fundamentally affect the social structure, the civilization, the culture about us. This is a fundamental question which most of us are unwilling to look at because we are so concerned with the education of the masses.

Now, is the individual different from the world? Isn't the individual, you and I, the total process of the world movement, world life? You and I are the result of the past—past thoughts, past actions. Not of any thought in particular, but the thought of human-kind. You are the result of the country, the culture, the civilization, the environmental and social influences, the religions, the climate. So is the individual "you" a separate, antagonistic process, an exclusive process away from the world, away from human culture, society?

When we talk about individual craving, individual will, individual attainment, what do we mean by the individual? Are you an individual because you have a little property, a name, a family, live in a separate house, and have peculiar idiosyncrasies and a different facial expression? Though we are dissimilar, is there not an extraordinarily great similarity between us all? After all, doesn't each one of us think more or less alike? Where is the individual, and where is the mass? Where is the demarcation between the two? I am not saying that there is not the individual, but I want to know from you, who insist on dividing the individual and the mass, where the line is between the two. We are all the result of the past; our thought is founded on the past, along with all the religious, organizational beliefs, and the orthodox traditions. Of all that, you are the result. Without that, you would not be an individual.

Is there an individuality exclusive from the world process, from the community process, from the society, from the world's organizational thoughts, feelings and beliefs? Then your transformation, not verbal but actual revolutionary transformation, will affect the world because you are the product of the world, the environment and society. But if you think you are an exclusive process unrelated to the world, to other people, then such a thought, which is the exclusive thought, will inevitably think, 'If I change, as I have no relationship to the other, I cannot possibly affect the world.' But if you are the product of the environment also, the effect, the result of a deeper process, which is not unrelated to the whole world process, then when you change, obviously you do affect the world.

We are affecting each other all the time, the world, the "you" and the "me" are influencing each other, modifying each other. So, you are not different from me. We have got the same passion, craving, pursuit and emotions. The same. All this exists because of our fear of not being individuals. But we are not individuals. I wish we were— then we would be able to think clearly for ourselves and not be persuaded by politicians, priests, executives and all the rest, to do what they tell us. If you were an individual, you would not seek a guru. We would throw away all the scum of gurus and wouldn't belong to any organization. But we are not individuals, despite our different faces and physiognomy. Inwardly, we are extraordinarily alike.

Are you and I not the result of each other's influence and relationship? Therefore, you and I exist only together. There is no such thing as isolation. And since you and I influence each other, you and I are not separate. Therefore I cannot exist without you, economically, socially or psychologically. I can be in isolation in an asylum without you, and that is what most of us are trying to do: create a character in isolation, which is a kind of asylum. Since you and I are related, since I cannot exist without you and you cannot exist without me, the "you" and the "me" is the whole world. Whether you live in Russia, North America, South America or Japan, you and I are the whole world.

Since we are the product, you and I, of each other's influence and the influence of another, are we individuals? How can we be individuals when we are influencing each other all the time, when I am the product of the past, and you are the product of the past, and the two pasts related in the present, modifying? How can we be individuals? There can only be individuality with aloneness, when you are not influenced by me and I am not influenced by you, psychologically and therefore externally. Until then, we are not individuals. That is why we have to become alone to find truth.

It is a clever invention on the part of the exploiter, on the part of the priest, the politician, the dictator, the ruler, the general, to treat individuals as the mass. It is so much more convenient. We do the same. But there is only you and me in relationship, which creates the society—the "you" and "me" all over the world. We, you and me, are constantly influencing each other. We are modifying each other. The past in conjunction with the present is producing you and me. We cannot dissociate ourselves from the past. We are the past, you and I.

Now, if you and I want to find what is true, must we not dissociate from all influence? I must have food, clothes and shelter; that has certain influences, and its organization has certain effects on me. That is an obvious fact, but when they become psychological, then I am enthralled; I am caught. In freedom only can we discover what is truth.

The past in relation to the present is the "me". There is no "me" without the past, and the "me" is the result of the past in conjunction with the present, and you likewise. So if I want to understand truth, reality, God, what you will, mustn't I be free from that past? This means my being alone from the net of influence, whether it is good or bad, free from nationalism and belief, which are all the effects outwardly of what you call the mass. Mustn't you be free, or mustn't the mind be untrammelled by those things you call belief, nationalism and all the rest of it, which are the effects of our relationship to each other and inward fear? These come into being when you seek security.

Don't you discover anything only when your mind is unoccupied, when it is unburdened? So, if you and I want to discover reality, mustn't you and I be free from the influences which, psychologically, we are constantly creating? Therefore, mustn't you be free from nationalism and class?

So, that is why it is essential to discuss this point very clearly and simply. Because the implications are tremendous. It means throwing over all the traditions, which are mere imitation, and re-examining the whole problem anew. Surely, you can examine the whole problem anew only when the intention to discover the truth is real. But if you are merely satisfied in your occupation, which makes you superior, makes you different, gives you the hereditary title of a Brahmin or an Englishman or a Russian, or an ideologist, then you have no problem. Then you will keep to your titles, your nationalities, your beliefs. But if you want to find truth, surely there must be freedom. Not freedom from relationship—I cannot be free from you; I depend on you for food, clothes, shelter, my physical existence—but freedom to investigate, to find. I cannot be free if psychologically I am bound to you. I am bound to you as long as I am seeking something from you psychologically. And because I am seeking something from you, I create a society that is disintegrating all the time.

Being influenced, being related to you, creates society. That society, which is the environment, again influences my children and me, and we are caught in the environmental influences. So I create a society with you, and then I am caught in it. But to investigate it, to find the truth of it, I must dissociate first. And this dissociation, I call, for the moment, aloneness. Therefore, one who is seeking truth must be free of the influence of society, not of relationship. How can I be free from you? I depend on you for food, clothes and shelter. But, if I am seeking truth, I won't use food, clothes and shelter as a means of self-expansion.

You and I have to create a new society. You and I, not the labels, are going to create a new culture, a new civilization. Systems have never created new cultures; only you and I can. The world is collapsing, the structure is disintegrating, and so you and I have to create a new culture. You and I are the salt of the earth, and it depends on you and me. That is why we must have a revolution, in you and me, in our thinking. It is a fact that the world is collapsing; it is not rhetorical.

There is no individual, and therefore you and I must become the individual—not the individual who is self-enclosed—to create this revolution in each of us, not tomorrow or the day after, nor in the days to come, but now. This thing must happen now, not tomorrow. And to happen now, you must be free from the influences that make you, that influence you into a pattern of action. You are merely patterns of action, not the actor who thinks clearly and sees and acts. You have to be both the master and the pupil. You have to become the architect as well as the player—you and I. We have done away with all leaders, all organizations. We have to restart the whole thing anew. Therefore, you and I have to become the whole thing, and we can only become the master and the pupil, builder and the architect when there is truth. But truth cannot come into being without freedom, and freedom means clarity.

When you love somebody, there is no individual, no you and me—there is only a state of being. That state of being is active; that state of being is action. And that alone is going to create a new world—not ideas, not plans, not systems. A state of being can only come when there is freedom, freedom from all that is false. And to see the false, there must be the true. You cannot see the false without truth—you can only see what is false when you see what is true.

§

Question: Why is it that in the balance of nature, there is always death and suffering?

Krishnamurti: Why is it we have killed fifty million whales? Fifty million. And still we are killing whales. We are killing every kind of species. The tigers are coming to an end; the cheetahs, the leopards and the elephants, for their tusks, for their flesh—you know all that. Are we not a much more dangerous animal than the rest of the animals? And you want to know why in nature there is death and suffering.

94

You see a tiger killing a cow or deer. That is the natural way of life. The moment we interfere, it becomes real cruelty. You have seen baby seals being knocked on the head, and when there is a great protest against it, they say they have to live that way.

So, where shall we start to understand the world about us and the world within us? The world within us is so enormously complex, but we want first to understand the world of nature, which becomes our mania. Perhaps if we could start with ourselves—not to hurt, not to be violent, not to be nationalistic, but to feel for the whole of humanity, then perhaps we shall have a proper relationship between ourselves and nature. Now we are destroying the earth, the air, the things of the sea. We are the greatest danger to the world.

§

Question: The whole world of nature is a competition to survive. Is it not innate in humans to struggle for the same reason? And are we not struggling against our basic nature in seeking to change?

Krishnamurti: Don't change. It is very simple. If you want to remain as you are, carry on; nobody is going to prevent you. Religions have tried to civilise humanity, but they haven't succeeded. On the contrary, some religions have killed more people than anybody on earth. We have had two appalling wars, and we have killed millions. And if we carry on this way, not wanting to change, then all right.

Nature struggles to achieve light, like in a forest, for example. And it is a struggle— in nature, the bigger and stronger animals kill the smaller and weaker. The tiger kills the deer; this goes on, part of nature. And the questioner says, if it is an intrinsic part of nature, why should we change at all?

Why do we say it's intrinsic? Why do we say that it is all right in nature and therefore it is all right with us too, so why bother to change? We say it is part of us, part of nature, part of our existence—intrinsically this is what we are. And if that is so, that it is instinct, that it is innate in us—which one questions very deeply—then I cannot change anything. But why do we accept that it is innate in us? Is it my indolence that says, 'For God's sake, leave it all alone'? Is it my sense of exhaustion?

Or, as human beings, we are supposed to be a little more intelligent, a little more reasonable, a little saner, and we are supposed to use our sanity, our intelligence, our experience to live differently. To live differently— perhaps that difference may be total. But we are now being encouraged to remain mediocre, through education and all the rest of it. So is it mediocrity that is fighting us, that we hold onto and say, 'We are slowly moving, it's all right'? We are slowly moving towards the precipice!

Begin to question the whole process of our existence, using common sense, logic, reason, awareness, intuition. One questions intuition because it may be one's wish-fulfilment, calling it instinct or intuition. One has to use logic in all this, not just say, 'But it is innate.'

EDUCATION AND WORLD PEACE

Why do we educate our children?

I do not know why we educate our children. We have perhaps never asked what the intention, the meaning of education is. Is it to turn out so many engineers, technicians, academics, professors and specialists? Apparently, that is what is happening—the cultivation of memory about facts, being technologically educated, so that human beings throughout the world can earn a livelihood, settle down in a particular pattern of society, and disregard our whole psychological structure. That is what is actually happening in the world: cultivating one fragment of the mind so that we go through school, college and university, if one wants to, and learn sufficient information, facts, and act from that memory, skilfully or not. That is the pattern set for us in education.

The psychological factors of human beings, because they are so utterly neglected, so disregarded, not thought about and gone into, have produced a lopsided and fragmented society. If that is the education most of us want, and that is what our children are educated to, then we must inevitably face the fact of conflicts, wars, terrorism and all the ugliness that is going on in the world.

So when we talk about education, what do we mean by it? Is it the cultivation not only of knowledge but also to be concerned with the total human? Isn't the concern of education not only the technical development of humanity, with considerable information and knowledge, but also the understanding of the whole psychological structure? The two should go together so that we are total human beings, not fragmented, broken beings.

The right kind of education is to give a totality to the comprehension of life

What happens when you have been through the mill of so-called education? When you come out of college, you are almost dead. You may breathe, your heart may work, but your mind, spirit, your sensitivity, your love of life has gone, trampled by the professors, teachers, by examinations, by everything. You come out a withered thing, like a branch that was once full, rich, pliant. You come out a dead thing, for you are only interested in getting a job, sex and having children. And then life is over. That is the tragedy of this so-called education.

Education has failed. It has failed because we are destroying one another. It has failed because we have more and more wars, threats, fear, tyranny. Do you know what is happening? Though you may have a B.A. or M.A. after your name and get a job as a clerk, minister, governor, teacher, you will be a dead thing, and a dead thing is useless. It cannot create a new world though it may mouth a lot of pleasant-sounding words. That is why it is very important while you are young—and do please understand this—to love, to pour your heart into something. And if you can maintain it through life, you will create a new world.

It all depends on what you want life to be. If you want to live merely as a glorified governor, with a lot of money, power and a car, you will have one kind of education. If you want to be a jet pilot with a marvellous feeling of freedom and danger, then you will have one kind of education. If you want to be an engineer, build a beautiful bridge, build waterworks, lay beautiful roads or build reservoirs, you will have one kind of education. And if you want to be a physicist, you will have one kind of education. If you want to be a clerk, you will have one kind of education. Life goes on like that, does it not?

This is the kind of education most people have, but that is not education at all. That is merely learning a job that will give you a livelihood. Any fool with a B.A. after their name can earn a livelihood— anybody. But life is not just that, is it? Life is much more vast; life is greater. The greater includes the lesser. That is, if life is beauty, if life is love, living a full, rich life, seeking the stars, enjoying yourself, playing sport, reading, your intellect fully matured, capable of thinking, and also if you know how to search out God and truth, then whether you are a clerk, a jet pilot or an engineer, is a very little affair. But we don't take the greater.

The earth is divided into America, England, Russia, India, Egypt and so on. It is divided, and we are all fighting over it. But the earth is ours, yours and mine. If you feel that, this sense of the earth, which is so marvellously beautiful and sustaining, if you feel for the whole of the earth as yours and mine, then it does not matter where you are from. This is education, not the passing of examinations and getting a job.

So, the cultivation of the mind and the heart is education. The cultivation of the mind requires a great deal of work, real hard work. You have to apply, you have to study, not only books but the life about you—the poverty, the farmworkers walking, the poor women carrying things on their head all day—to know all that is part of education. Without knowing all that, to pass a silly examination and get a job has no meaning because you don't help create a new world. And a new world must come into being, otherwise we are going to end in misery, frustration and sorrow.

To have a new education, a new kind of outlook on life so that you not only pass examinations but also are highly sensitive to life, to look at the trees, to listen to the frogs, to enjoy yourself, to smile at the sky, to be free—you understand what that means? We generally don't get that kind of education. In what you call education, there is nothing new. That is the old game, that is the old education of centuries.

Now, what can there be that is new? We must learn mathematics, geography, history; that is part of education, part of learning. But how you learn is where real education comes because you can destroy your mind by learning geography, history and mathematics. Your mind can become merely routine, a repetitive machine. Or your mind in learning can become extraordinarily expansive, alive, alert, because life is a process of learning.

There was a painter, one of the greatest in the world. When he was 90, he painted a picture and wrote a bit about it, saying that he was still learning at 90 how to paint. To keep on learning so that your mind is always pliable, always alive, eager, to know, to inquire, to face dangers, to be in revolt, not to accept authority—all that requires an extraordinary mind. This must be cultivated. Not writing and mathematics only, but the cultivation of a mind capable of great sensitivity and comprehension to find out what truth, God and the beauty of life is. That is the function of the right kind of education: to give a totality to the comprehension of life.

Question: Why do you think we are insensitive to life? Is it not due to the occupation with ourselves?

Krishnamurti: First of all, do you know what it is to be sensitive? To be sensitive means to be sensitive to beauty and to ugliness—not just to beauty alone but to the squalor and the misery; to the animals, how they are treated, to the village that is rotting—to be sensitive to that as well as to the river, the beauty of the trees, the birds, the sky; to be sensitive like a photographic plate that takes in the ugly things as well as the beautiful; to be so sensitive that you photograph everything in your mind. If you discard one and accept the other, you lose sensitivity. That is what I mean by sensitivity; others may mean something else.

Does not that sensitivity become dull when the mind is occupied with its own self? Obviously. When you are worried, when you are unhappy, when you want to be a great person, when you are thinking about yourself, your wife or your husband or your little job, occupied, then you don't see anything around you.

Do you, as you go about, notice anything? Do you notice the caterpillar, the butterfly, the person on the road? Do you notice any of that? You don't because you are so occupied with yourself, your games, laughter, work, sports, etc. Your mind gradually becomes so occupied with itself that you lose all sensitivity. And a mind that is so occupied, so isolated, becomes astonishingly miserable. Being miserable, you then read the Gita or follow a leader, hoping to get rid of misery, but you cannot.

Question: How is it possible to get rid of these worldly occupations?

Krishnamurti: Now, what do you call worldly occupations? What do you think is worldly occupation—to be occupied with money, sex, having a better house, a better job? You would call that worldly occupation, would you not? Now, you call that worldly occupation, but someone who reads the Gita all day, chants, thinks about God and practises virtue, who says, 'I must be kind, I must be good, I must be humble,' they are also occupied. But such occupation you call unworldly. One you call worldly, but a mind occupied with God, with doing good, with virtue, with reading the Gita or something else, you call that spiritual. To me, both are worldly because, in both, the mind is occupied—occupied with so-called worldly things and so-called spiritual things.

When the mind is occupied with this or with that, such a mind is incapable of finding out what truth is or what God is. The mind that is not occupied, because it understands the whole process of occupation, only such a mind can understand. Mind is occupied because it is frightened not to be occupied. That is one of the reasons. Also, occupation implies an activity with itself, with the things that are concerning itself. Such a mind is an occupied mind.

You know, a cup is only useful when it is empty. You can fill it. But a cup that is already full, what value has it? Similarly, your mind is already full, whether with so-called worldly things or with so-called spiritual things. It is already full; it is already occupied. There is no space. The mind that is really empty, because it understands the full significance of what it is to be occupied, such a mind alone can find out. Such a mind is spiritual, not the other mind.

Education is something entirely different: a mind in revolution

Education is the capacity to help you to meet life. Life is an enormous thing, really a marvellous thing with extraordinary joy, with great depth of sorrow, great beauty, great love, and the extraordinary excitement of living. And to meet that, you have to have the capacity not merely to pass examinations but to meet it so that your mind is equally great as life. Cultivate the mind, plough the mind so that it has no limitation and does not think about itself everlastingly.

No one is going to help you, neither your parents nor your teachers, which is a sad thing—they are all frightened, and they want things to go on as they are. So you have not to look to anybody for help, which is a very hard thing, especially while you are young. Do realise this; I am telling you very seriously from the bottom of my heart that no one is going to help you. On the contrary, they will make you conform, make you adjust to what they think is the right society, which is this hideous society of poverty, war, hate and all the nonsense they talk about religion which they don't mean.

So you have to work, look to yourself so that your mind is cultivated and has the depth to meet life. You have to study very hard, not just learn examples, remember dates and be able to write essays. Your mind is made intelligent by discussion, by talking, and by reading books in addition to the prescribed curricular books. You are not only to study every day to sharpen your mind, your wit and your heart, but also you have to see the poor people around you.

You know, you cannot live by yourself in this world. People try to; they try to enclose themselves by walls in a house or with ideas, but you cannot live alone in this world. Nothing exists in this world by itself. Everything is interrelated. Living alone is impossible because you depend upon me, and I upon you, for your clothes, food and shelter. You depend on the milkman, the postman, the railway clerk, but inwardly don't depend on anybody. Psychologically, inwardly, be like a tower to yourself. Otherwise, your life becomes utterly empty, stupid, has no meaning.

Education is not merely the cultivation of memory. You study, the examiner asks you some questions, and you reply with what you remember. This is called education. That is not education; education is something entirely different: a mind in revolution. Then when you look at a tree or a bird on the telephone wire, you have immediate communication with them. They are lovely things. They quicken the insight, sharpen the mind and give depth to the heart. Then life becomes a very rich thing, a marvellous thing, not a hideous thing where people are kept down or are slaves to something. This needs a revolution.

So education is really another form of making the mind remain in revolution, in revolt. But not revolt against petty society. Revolution only comes when you step out of society, when you are no longer driven by ambition, by your vanity, or the tradition. When you step out of that narrowness, there is revolution. And that is the only revolution that matters.

It is a most extraordinary thing in life to be religious, really religious, not going to temples or following some Guru, which is just vanity. I assure you that is nothing else but vanity, conceit in the form of self-improvement. Religion is something entirely different, not putting ashes on your forehead or bathing in the Ganges, but to feel deeply, love deeply, suffer deeply and be free of suffering, and not belong to this society at all. You have to put on clothes, but that is not belonging to society. To belong to society is to be ambitious, vain, greedy, tradition-bound, fearful. That is what it means to belong to society, but the moment you are not greedy, when there is no fear, when there is no ambition, then you are out of it. To be free from society is right education. Then you will find that life is an extraordinary thing, so vast, so creative and with a love that passes all understanding.

You know, you are attentive now for a few minutes, but when you go outside, you forget all this, at least some of you. The older people naturally will because they are occupied, busy complying with the rule of government, to keep things going without any disturbance. But those of you who listen will take this to your heart and play with it, go with it to the end, so that life is rich, immense and beautiful.

8

CAN THE HUMAN BEING COMPLETELY CHANGE?

The future of humanity is at stake

It is important that you and the speaker establish right relationship. He is not a guru. He is not going to inform you what to think, how to think, but together we are going to observe the activities of human beings right throughout the world, why they have become what they are: cruel, destructive, violent, idealistic, and, in the world of technology, doing astonishing things of which most of us are unaware; why after thousands of years of wars, shedding tears, human beings behave in this manner.

We have divided the world into nationalities; we have divided the world into Catholic, Protestant, Hindu, Muslim, and so on, religiously. Where there is division, as the Arab and the Jew, the Hindu and the Muslim, there must be conflict. This is a natural law and what is actually taking place in the world. Why is there this division? Who has brought it about? Why have we become what we are despite great experience, despite great knowledge, despite vast technological advancement? Why have we remained more or less what we have been for millennia?

Is it because our mind, our brain, is programmed, like a computer? Professionals program the computer, and it can repeat more rapidly than we can, giving infinite information. Is it that every human being in the world has also been programmed, to be an Indian, a Muslim, a Hindu, and so on?

Is your brain programmed, thinking in a conventional, narrow, limited way? Our brain is limited, but it has the capacity for extraordinary invention, extraordinary technological advancement. Perhaps most of us do not know what is actually going on in the biological world, in the technological world, in the world of warfare, because most of us are concerned with our daily living, with our own particular problems, with our own fulfilments. So we generally forget the vast advancement humanity is making in one direction, in the technological world, and completely neglect the psychological world, the world of human behaviour, the world of consciousness.

What are the causes of all this? Why have human beings been programmed as Christians for two thousand years, believing in certain doctrines, seeking one saviour, and the Muslim programmed for the last thousand or more years to believe in certain principles, and the Hindu being programmed perhaps for the last three to five thousand years? So our brains are conditioned. Does one ever realize how our brain is acting, thinking, looking? Where there is limitation, there must be conflict.

Our brains are conditioned to be this or that, to behave in a certain manner, to enjoy, to suffer, to have a great burden of fear, uncertainty, confusion, and the ultimate fear of death. We are conditioned to that, and there are those professors, scholars, writers who say that the human brain will always be conditioned; it can never be free; you can modify that conditioning by environmental influence, by law. They say it can be modified, changed here and there, but the human brain can never actually be free. Please understand the implication of that. Therefore, totalitarian governments are controlling human thought and not allowing people to think freely. And if people do, they are sent to the psychiatric ward or concentration camps.

It is most important to find out for yourself whether the human brain, conditioned through experience and knowledge, can ever be free, have no fear, no conditioning. Where there is conditioning, there must be conflict, because all conditioning is limited.

Are you aware of your own thinking, your own reactions, your own responses, how they are limited, how they are conditioned, how you depend on past knowledge? See how life becomes very narrow, rather sloppy, confused, with the fear of insecurity. If one is aware of all one's inward activities, thoughts, feelings and reactions, you will find out for yourself how conditioned you are and how limited you are. When you recognize that fact, you realize the consequences of that conditioning, that limitation. Wherever there is limitation, for example, as Hindu or Muslim, there must be conflict. Wherever there is a division between husband and wife, there must be conflict. And human beings throughout the world, after all this evolution, are still in conflict with each other.

Please consider all this because we are concerned with your life as a human being. And that life, your daily living, has become extraordinarily complex, extraordinarily dangerous, difficult and uncertain. The future of humanity really is at stake. This is not a threat; this is not a pessimistic point of view. The crisis is not only physical, it is in our consciousness, in our being.

So in talking over together, become aware of all this. In becoming aware, you begin to discover; you begin to find out for yourself how your life has become such pain, such anxiety, such uncertainty. If you are so aware, you can proceed more deeply, but if you merely listen to the words, the words have very little meaning. Words have a certain significance, but if one lives in words, as most people do, in symbols, in myths and in romantic nonsense, we make life more difficult, more and more dangerous for each other. So please listen to find out, question and doubt, so that your brain becomes aware of itself.

We are asking why human beings, who have developed the most marvellous technology the world has ever known, have remained more or less the same psychologically, inwardly. We have systems, we have ideals, we have all the so-called sacred books, but we have not radically brought about a change, a psychological revolution. So is it possible to bring about a total mutation in the brain cells themselves?

We are talking about the radical change of human behaviour so that we are not self-centred as we are now, which is causing such great destruction in the world. If one is aware, we can ask whether that conditioning can be totally changed so that humanity is completely free.

Now we think we are free to do what we like. Each individual thinks they can do what they like, and that freedom is based on choice. We can choose where to live, what kind of work we do, choose between this idea and that idea, this ideal or that ideal, change from one god to another god, from one guru to another, from one philosopher to another. This capacity to choose brings in the concept of freedom. But choice is not freedom. Choice is merely moving in the same field from one corner to another. Being limited, is it possible for the brain to free itself so that there is no fear? Then there is right relationship with all the neighbours in the world.

Now we are going to inquire into the nature of our consciousness. Your consciousness is what you are: your beliefs, your ideals, your gods, violence, fear, romantic concepts, your pleasure, your sorrow, the fear of death and the everlasting question, which has been there from time immemorial, whether there is something sacred beyond all this. That is your consciousness. That is what you are; you are not different from your consciousness. Can that content of consciousness be transformed, be totally changed?

First, your consciousness is not yours. Your consciousness is the consciousness of all humanity because what you think, your beliefs, sensations, reactions, pain, sorrow, insecurity, gods and so on, are shared by all humanity. Go to America, Europe, Russia or China, and you will find that human beings suffer. They are frightened of death; they have beliefs, they have ideals. They speak a particular language, but their thinking, reactions and responses are generally shared by all human beings. It is a fact that you suffer and your neighbour suffers. That neighbour may be thousands of miles away, but they suffer. They are as insecure as you are. They may have a lot of money, but inwardly there is insecurity. The rich people in America, or those in power, all go through this pain, anxiety, loneliness and despair.

So, your consciousness is not yours any more than your thinking is. It is not individual thinking. Thinking is common from the poorest, the most uneducated, unsophisticated, in a tiny village, to the most sophisticated brain. The great scientists all think. The thinking may be more complex, but thinking is general, shared by all human beings. Therefore, it is not your individual thinking. This is rather difficult to see, and to recognize the truth of it, because we are so conditioned as individuals. All your religious books, whether Christian, Muslim or another, sustain and nourish this idea, this concept of an individual. You have to question that. You have to find out the truth of the matter.

We are investigating together, and we see that human consciousness is similar, shared by all human beings. Therefore there is no individual. Someone may be more educated than you, may be taller or shorter; the outside may be different, but inwardly we share the ground of all humanity. This is a fact. But if you are caught in the conditioning of being an individual, you will never understand the immensity and extraordinary fact that you are the entire humanity.

From that there is love, compassion and intelligence. But if you are merely conditioned to the idea that you are an individual, you have endless complications because it is based on illusion, not fact. The illusion may be of thousands of years, but it is still an illusion.

You are the result of your environment; you are the result of the language you speak, the food you eat, the clothes, the climate, the tradition handed down from generation to generation—you are all that. You are the product of the society which you have created. Society is not different from you. We have created the society, the society of greed, envy, hatred, brutality, violence, wars; we have created all that, and we have also created the extraordinary world of technology. So, you are the world, and the world is you. Your consciousness is not yours; it is the ground on which all human beings stand and all human beings think. So, you are actually not an individual. That is one of the realities, a truth that one must understand.

Do not accept what the speaker is saying but question your own isolation, because *individual* means isolation. To separate oneself from another is isolation, like nations isolate themselves. And they think that in isolation there is security. There is no security in isolation. But the governments of the world, representing the people of each country, are maintaining isolation, and therefore they are perpetuating wars. If you recognize the truth, the fact that you are not an individual, that inwardly there is no division, that we all share the same problems, then the question is: can you, as a human being representing all humanity, bring about a fundamental, psychological revolution?

You might ask, 'If I change, will it affect in any way the rest of humanity?' If I change, if there is a change in a particular person, how will it affect the whole consciousness of humanity? Please do put that question to yourself. Even as a single, isolated human being, you are asking, 'If I change, what effect has it in the world?'

If you change fundamentally, you affect the whole consciousness of humanity. Napoleon affected the whole consciousness of Europe. Stalin affected the whole consciousness of Russia. The Christian Saviour has affected the consciousness of the world, and the Hindus, with their peculiar gods, have affected the consciousness of the world. When you as a human being radically transform psychologically, that is, be free of fear, have right relationship with each other, end sorrow, and so on, which is a radical transformation, you affect the whole consciousness of humanity. It is not an individual affair. It is not a selfish affair. It is not individual salvation. It is the salvation of all human beings, of which you are one.

We must also inquire what relationship is. Why is there, in human relationship with each other, such conflict, misery, and an intense sense of loneliness? From history, from all the knowledge that has been acquired, studied, we see we have lived in conflict with each other. Relationship is existence: without relationship you cannot exist. In that existence, there is conflict. Relationship is absolutely necessary. Life is relationship; action is relationship; what you think brings about relationship or destroys relationship.

Why do human beings live in conflict with each other, why is there is conflict between you and your husband or wife? Where there is conflict in relationship, there is no love, there is no compassion, and there is no intelligence. Are you actually related? You may be related to a man or woman sexually, but apart from that, are you related to anybody? Relation means non-isolation. There is the one who goes to the office every day, to a factory, to some form of occupation, leaving the house at 8 o'clock, spending the whole day working, for so many years, and then dies. And there is the one who is ambitious, greedy, envious, struggling, competing; they come home, and the partner is also competitive, jealous, anxious, going on in their own way. They may meet sexually, talk together, care somewhat, but they remain separate, like two railway lines never meeting. This is what we call relationship, which is an actuality. The perpetual division between two people is a fact of life, each holding on to their opinions and conclusions.

The fact is, however intimate that relationship may be, there is always conflict, one dominating the other, one possessing the other, one jealous of the other. Now, can that relationship be totally changed? Ask yourself this.

Why is there a conflict between two human beings, whether they are highly educated or not at all educated? They may be great scientists, but they are ordinary human beings, like you and another—fighting, quarrelling, ambitious. Why does this state exist? Is it not because each person is concerned about themselves? We are isolating ourselves, and in isolation you cannot have the right relationship.

You hear this, but you will not do anything about it because we fall into a habit, into a rut, into a groove, into a narrow little life, and we put up with it, however miserable, unhappy, quarrelsome or ugly it is. But please inquire, question, doubt whether it is possible to live with another in complete harmony without any dissension or division. If you really, deeply inquire, you will find that you have created an image about your wife or husband, and they have created an image about you. Each has built an image, a picture about the other. These two pictures, images, are in relationship with each other. Where there is an image about another, there must be conflict.

I am quite sure you all have an image about the speaker. Why? You don't know the speaker. You can never know the speaker, but you have created an image about him: that he is religious, nonreligious, he is stupid or clever, he is beautiful, he is this or that. And with that image, you look at the person. But the image is not the person. The image is the reputation, and reputations are easily created, good or bad. The human brain, thought, creates the image. The image is the conclusion, and we live by images and imagination.

The making of pictures has no place in love. We don't love each other; we may hold hands, sleep together, do this and ten different things, but we have no love for each other. If you had that quality, that perfume of love, there would be no wars. There would be no Hindu and Muslim, Jew and Arab. But you listen to all this and remain with your images. You still wrangle with each other, quarrel with each other. Your life has become so extraordinarily meaningless.

I wonder how many of us realize that we are put together by thought. Your gods are put together by thought. All the rituals, dogmas, and philosophies are put together by thought, and thought is not sacred. Thought is always limited. Thought has created an image about you as the audience, about you as the wife or husband, about you as an Indian and he as an American, and so on. It is these images, which are unreal, that are dividing humanity. You should never call yourself Indian, Russian, American: we are human beings.

Then we should have no wars. We should have a global government, a global relationship. But you are not interested in all that. You hear all this, and if you don't change radically, you are bringing about destruction to future generations. So, please give ear, thought and attention to what is going on outside you and what is going on inwardly, for the inward psyche conquers the outer environment.

We give such importance to the outer. We must have right society, right laws, feed the poor, and be concerned about the poor, but the inward thought, inward feeling and inward isolation are separating us, and you are responsible for this. Each one is responsible for this. Unless you change fundamentally, inwardly, the future is very dangerous. Unless you fundamentally bring about a change in your daily life, have right relationship with each other, live correctly, not be ambitious and so on, there is no possibility of ending conflict between human beings.

My responsibility is not to have an image

Krishnamurti: What is the responsibility of a human being in relationship? Relationship is life. Relationship is the foundation of existence. Relationship is absolutely necessary; otherwise, you cannot exist. Relationship means co-operation. Relation means love and generosity –everything is involved in that one word. Now what is human responsibility in relationship?

Questioner: If we were genuinely and completely sharing, responsibility would be fully present.

K: Yes, but how does it express itself in relationship? Not only between you and me, now, but between man and woman, between neighbours – relationship to everything, to nature. What is my relationship to nature? Would I go and kill baby seals? Would I destroy human beings, calling them enemies? Would I destroy nature, everything we are doing now? We are destroying the earth, the air, the sea, everything – because we feel totally irresponsible.

Q: We see what is out there as something to operate on.

K: So I ask, how does this responsibility show itself in my life? Suppose I am married – what is my responsibility? Am I related to my wife?

Q: The record doesn't seem very good.

K: Not only record, the actuality. Am I related to my wife? Or am I related to my wife according to the image I make about her? And I am responsible for that image?

Q: Yes, because my input has been continuous with respect to that image.

K: So I have no relationship with my wife if I have an image about her. Or if I have an image about myself when I want to be successful, and all the rest of that business.

Q: Since we were talking about now, being now, there is a point of contact between what you are saying and the phrase you used in one of our earlier conversations, the betrayal of the present.

K: Absolutely. You see, that is the whole point, sir. If I am related to you, I have no image about you, or you have no image about me, then we have relationship. We have no relationship if I have an image about myself or about you.

Our images have a relationship, so in actuality we have no relationship. I might sleep with my wife, but it is not a relationship. It is physical contact, sensory excitement, nothing else. My responsibility is not to have an image.

This is really quite important, because, go where you will, there is no relationship between human beings. That is the tragedy, and from that arises all our conflicts, violence, the whole business. So when there is this responsibility, the feeling of this responsibility, it translates itself in relationship. It doesn't matter with whom. There is freedom from the known, which is the image. In that freedom, goodness flowers. And that is the beauty. Beauty is not an abstract thing, but it goes with goodness – goodness in behaviour, goodness in conduct, goodness in action.

Q: Sometimes, while we have been talking, I have started a sentence with *if*, and I have looked into your eyes, and immediately knew I had said the wrong thing. We are always "iffing" it up.

K: "Iffing" it up! I know, sir. We are always dealing with abstractions rather than with reality.

Q: Immediately we "if" a construction is out there which we endlessly talk about.

K: That's right.

Q: And we get cleverer and cleverer about it, and it has nothing to do with anything.

K: So, how does this responsibility translate itself in human behaviour? You follow, sir?

Q: There would be an end to violence.

K: Absolutely.

Q: It wouldn't taper off.

K: You see what we have done? Sexually, morally, in every way, we are violent human beings, and not being able to resolve this, we have created an ideal of not being violent. This means there is the fact – violence – and abstraction from the fact, which is non-fact, and we try to live the non-fact.

Q: Yes, and immediately that produces conflict because it cannot be done.

K: Conflict, misery, confusion, all that. Why does the mind do it? The mind does it because it doesn't know what to do with the fact of violence. Therefore, in abstracting the idea of not being violent, it postpones action. I am trying not to be violent, and in the meantime, I am jolly well violent.

Q: Yes.

K: And this is an escape from the fact. All abstractions are an escape from the fact. So the mind does it because it is incapable of dealing with the fact, or it doesn't want to deal with the fact, or it is lazy and says, 'I will try to do it another day.' All this is involved when it withdraws from the fact.

Now, in the same way, the fact is our relationship is non-existent. I may say to my wife, 'I love you,' but relationship is non-existent because I have an image about her, and she has an image about me. So we have lived on abstractions.

Q: It occurs to me that the word *fact* itself, about which there has been no end of disquisitions ...

K: Oh yes, of course. The fact, what is – let's call it *what is*. You see, this reveals a tremendous lot. When you feel responsible, you feel responsible for the education of your children – not only yours, but all children. Are you educating them to conform to society? Are you educating them to merely acquire a job? Are you educating them to the continuity of what has been? Are you educating them to live in abstractions, as we are doing now?

So what is your responsibility as a father or mother, it doesn't matter who you are, for the education of a human being? What is your responsibility, if you feel responsible, for human growth, human culture, human goodness? What is your responsibility to the earth? It is a tremendous thing to feel responsible. And also, with responsibility goes love, care, attention.

Q: Yes. I was going to ask you about care in relation to responsibility – something that would flow immediately.

K: Naturally. That involves a great deal too because the mother depends on the child and the child depends on the mother or father or whoever it is. So that dependence is cultivated, not only on the father and the mother but on a teacher, on somebody to tell you what to do, on your guru.

Gradually the child is incapable of standing alone, and therefore later they depend on their partner for comfort, for sex, for this, that, and the other thing. They are lost without them. They are lost without a guru or teacher. It becomes so ridiculous.

But when the feeling of responsibility exists, all this disappears. You are responsible for your behaviour, for the way you bring up your children, for the way you treat a dog, a neighbour, nature—everything is in your hands. Therefore you have to become astonishingly careful about what you do. Careful, not, 'I must not do this, I must do that,' but care, which means affection, consideration, diligence. All that goes with responsibility, which present-day society denies.

The various gurus imported into the West are creating such mischief, making those unfortunate, thoughtless people who want excitement join them and do all kinds of ridiculous nonsensical things.

So, to come back: freedom implies responsibility. And therefore, freedom means care, diligence, not negligence.

§

Unless there is a change, there will always be war. So our question is: how can the brain and mind—that is, the total human being—physiologically, neurologically, completely change? How can the human being completely change? Such a change is necessary—one sees that. And unless there is a change, there will always be war: one nation against another, the terrible brutality of war, the linguistic differences, the economic differences, the social differences, the moral differences and the everlasting battle, outward and inward. So there must be change. Now, how is one to bring it about?

Please see the extraordinary complexity of this question, what is involved in it. We have tried so many ways—gone away to monasteries, renounced the world, gone into the woods and meditated, fasted, became celibate—we have done everything we could imagine—mesmerized ourselves, forced ourselves, examined, analysed our consciousness, the conscious and the unconscious—we have done everything to try to bring about a radical revolution within ourselves. And we have been ruthless in ourselves, as individuals and as human beings.

The two are entirely different. The individual is a local entity: a Parsi, a Buddhist, a Muslim and so on. The individual is conditioned by the environment. But the human being is beyond that, concerned with the total humanity—not about their country, linguistic differences, little wars and quarrels, petty little gods and so on, but concerned with the whole state of humanity, the conflict and despair.

When you see the whole, you can understand the particular. But the particular cannot possibly understand the whole. So, for the constantly introspective individual, inquiry has no meaning at all because they are still concerned with the pattern of their existence, conditioned by society, which includes religion and all the rest of it. Whereas a human being has lived for two million years—has suffered, has thought, has inquired, has borne, whether in Russia, China, America or India, and has done everything to bring about a radical change, yet fundamentally has not changed at all. We are what we have been for two million years!

The animal is very strong in us. The animal, with all its greed, envy, ambition, anger and ruthlessness, still exists deep down in our hearts and mind. And we have, through religion, through culture, through civilization, polished the outer. Perhaps a few of us have better manners. We know a little more: technologically, we have gone very far. We can discuss Western and Eastern philosophy, literature, we can travel all over the world, but inwardly, deep down, the roots are very firmly embedded.

Seeing all this, how is one—you as a human being and I as a human being—to change? Certainly not through tears, certainly not through intellection, not through following an ideological utopia, not through external tyranny, nor self-imposed tyranny. So one discards all this, and I hope you have also discarded it.

To discard one's nationality, one's gods, one's traditions, one's beliefs, to discard all the things that we have been brought up to believe in—to discard all this is a very difficult thing to do. We may intellectually agree, but deep down in the unconscious there is insistence on the importance of the past, to which we cling.

It is not a matter of saving your own particular little soul

It is not a revolution within oneself as an individual that we are talking about—a matter of saving your own particular little soul—but a revolution within oneself as a human being totally related to all other human beings.

124

We may consciously separate ourselves into petty individualities, but deep down, unconsciously, we are the inherited human experience of all time. Mere superficial changes on the economic or social level, though they may provide a little more comfort and convenience, are not productive of a new society. We are concerned not only with the human being's transformation of their total nature but also with bringing about a different society, a good society. And a good society is not possible if there are no good human beings.

Cultivating your backyard won't do very much

Question: What effect does a revolution in the mind of a single person have on the whole human race?

Krishnamurti: The individual is the local entity, the American, the Russian, the Indian—the local, conditioned, modern entity. The human being is much older. If there is a mutation in the human mind, will it affect the whole consciousness, not only of the individual but of humanity?

There are several things involved in this question: first, how to change society. You see that society must be changed, but how? Is it possible? Realizing the vested interests of the politicians, of the army, of the priests, of business, is it possible?

You are society, psychologically. You have created this society; you are part of it. The psychological structure of society is what you have psychologically created. It is not something different from you. You have conflict; your life, your daily existence is a battlefield; and the battlefields in wars are the extension of your daily life. You say, 'I want to change all that,' but can it be changed, or should you be concerned with the total human being who is two million years old? If there can be a mutation there, then everything will come right.

Merely changing a local entity, the individual, is not going to affect it a great deal. Cultivating your backyard isn't going to do very much. But when you are concerned with all humanity, then in that mutation of the psyche, perhaps the mutation will affect society.

It is because we function as localized entities that we are destroying ourselves

Question: What you are really telling us is to cultivate a private state of mind. I stress the word private. But the point is that we do have to live in the material world. Surely the active world can destroy our private state of mind.

Krishnamurti: I am not talking of the private mind at all. Our minds are the result of the totality of the human mind. We are the result of the society in which we live. This society has been created by each one of us. So the many are the "me", and the "me" is the many. There is no division between me and the many; I am the result of all that. However, I think we should differentiate between the individual and the human being.

The individual is the localized entity, the Englishman, the Indian, the American and so on, localized, conditioned by the locality, the culture, the climate, the food, the clothing. The human being is conditioned on a much larger scale. They belong to the whole world. Our sufferings, anxieties and fears are the same as those of an Indian who goes through terrible states, just like everyone else in the world. If we understand that, then the private cultivation of one's own mind also disappears. We are concerned with the total structure of the human mind, not our own minds, our little backyards, which are nothing. Our little backyards are as filthy as any other backyard or as clean as any other backyard.

My action then is not outside the world but in the world. All the time, I am here. What I am doing as a human being, going to the office, living with my family, I am aware of not as a private individual but as a human being. When I am aware of that as a human being, surely I am affecting the whole of the human mind. It is because we function as localized entities that we are destroying ourselves.

At present, India is going through a terrible period of starvation and hardship. The question is not an Indian question; it is a human question. The politicians won't see that; they want to keep their localities intact, their power, their position, their prestige. But they won't solve the problem that way. It is a human problem; it is a world problem, and we have to deal with it as a whole world, not as Indians or Americans or English, giving food or not giving food.

Action as a human being is entirely different from the action of a localized entity. The localized entity creates more harm, creates misery, as does the human being who is still caught in the human or animalistic struggle. Only the human being who has understood this whole

127

structure, its anxieties and agonies, can bring about a totally different kind of action.

Is it possible to live a life that is completely free from all conflict?

Is it possible for there to be no conflict at all, right through one's life? Traditionally, one accepts that there must be conflict, struggle, an everlasting fight, not only physiologically to survive, but psychologically in desire and fear, like and dislike, and so on. To live without conflict is to live a life without any effort, a life in which there is peace.

For centuries upon centuries, we have lived a life of battle, conflict both outwardly and inwardly, a constant struggle to achieve and fear of losing, dropping back. One may talk endlessly about peace, but there will be no peace as long as one is conditioned to the acceptance of conflict. If one says it is possible to live in peace, it is just an idea and therefore valueless. And if one says it is not possible, one blocks any investigation.

Go into it psychologically first, which is more important than physiologically. If one understands the nature and structure of conflict very deeply, psychologically, and perhaps ends it there, one may be able to deal with the physiological factor. But if one is only concerned with the physiological, biological factor of survival, then one probably will not be able to do it at all.

Why is there conflict, psychologically? From ancient times, both socially and religiously, there has been a division between the good and the bad. Is there really this division at all, or is there only what is, without its opposite? Suppose there is anger; that is the fact, that is what is, but 'I will not be angry' is an idea, not a fact. One never questions this division; one accepts it because one is traditional by habit, not wanting anything new. But there is a further factor: the division between the observer and the observed.

When one looks at a mountain, one looks at it as an observer and calls it a mountain. But the word is not the thing. The word *mountain* is not the mountain, but to oneself the word is very important. When one looks, instantly there is the response: 'That is a mountain.' Now, can one look at the thing called mountain without the word? Because the word is a factor of division. When one says, 'My wife' or 'My husband,' the word *my* creates division. The word, the name, is part of thought. When one looks at a man or woman, a mountain or tree, whatever it is, division takes place when thought, the name, the memory, comes into being.

Can one observe without the observer, who is the essence of all the memories, experiences, reactions and so on, which are from the past? If one looks at something without the word and memories, one looks without the observer. When one does that, there is only the observed, and there is no division and no conflict psychologically. Can one look at one's wife or husband, or one's intimate friend, without the name, the word and all the experiences that one has gathered in that relationship? When one so looks, one is looking at them for the first time.

Is it possible to live a life that is completely free from all psychological conflict? One has observed the fact; it will do everything if one lets the fact alone. There must be everlasting conflict as long as there is division between the image-making observer and the fact. That is a law. That conflict can be ended.

When there is an ending of psychological conflict—which is part of suffering—how does that apply to one's livelihood, how does that apply in one's relationship with others? How does the ending of psychological struggle, with all its conflict, pain, anxiety and fear, apply to one's daily living, one's daily going to the office, etc.? If it is a fact that one has ended psychological conflict, how will one live a life without conflict outwardly? When there is no conflict inside, there is no conflict outside because there is no division between the inner and the outer. It is like the ebb and flow of the sea. It is an absolute, irrevocable fact, which nobody can touch. It is inviolate.

If that is so, what shall one do to earn a livelihood? Because there is no conflict, there is no ambition. Because there is no conflict, there is no desire to be something. Because inwardly there is something absolute that is inviolate, which cannot be touched, which cannot be damaged, one does not depend psychologically on another. Therefore, there is no conformity, no imitation. So, not having all that, one is no longer heavily conditioned to success and failure in the world of money, position and prestige.

If one denies what is and creates the ideal of what should be, there is conflict. But to observe what actually is means one has no opposite, only what is. If you observe violence and use the word *violence* there is already conflict. The very word is already warped: there are people who approve of violence and people who do not. The whole philosophy of nonviolence is warped, both politically and religiously. There is violence, and its opposite: non-

130

violence. The opposite exists because you know violence. The opposite has its root in violence. One thinks that by having an opposite, by some extraordinary method or means, one will get rid of what is.

Now, can one put away the opposite and just look at violence, the fact? Nonviolence is not a fact. Nonviolence is an idea, a concept, a conclusion. The fact is violence—that one is angry, that one hates somebody, that one wants to hurt people, that one is jealous. All that is the implication of violence; that is the fact. Now, can one observe that fact without introducing its opposite? For then one has the energy—which was being wasted in trying to achieve the opposite—to observe what is. In that observation, there is no conflict.

So, what will one do who has understood this extraordinary complex existence based on violence, conflict, struggle? One who is actually free of it, not theoretically but actually free, which means no conflict—what will they do in the world? Will one ask this question if one is inwardly, psychologically, completely free from conflict? Obviously not. Only the one in conflict says, 'If there is no conflict, I will be at an end, I will be destroyed by society because society is based on conflict.' If one is aware of one's consciousness, what is one? If one is aware, one will see that one's consciousness is—in its absolute sense—in total disorder. It is contradictory, saying one thing, doing something else, always wanting something. The total movement is within an area that is confined and without space, and in that little space, there is disorder.

Are you different from your consciousness, or are you that consciousness? One is that consciousness. Then are you aware that you are in total disorder? Ultimately, that disorder leads to neurosis, so we have all the specialists in modern society, such as psychoanalysts, psychotherapists, etc.

Inwardly, is one in order, or is there disorder? Can one observe this fact? And what takes place when one observes choicelessly, which means without any distortion? Where there is disorder, there must be conflict. Where there is absolute order, there is no conflict. There is an absolute order that can only come about naturally, easily, without any conflict, when one is aware of oneself as a consciousness, aware of the confusion, the turmoil, the contradiction, outwardly and inwardly, observing without any distortion. Then out of that comes naturally, sweetly, easily, an order which is irrevocable.

The only true revolution is freeing the mind from its conditioning

Can we consider this, not as a collective group experiencing something, which is comparatively easy, but as individuals, can we inquire and find out for ourselves to what degree and depth we are conditioned? Can we be aware of that conditioning without any reaction to it, without condemning it or trying to alter it, without substituting new conditioning for the old, but be aware so easily and deeply that the very process of conditioning— which is, after all, the desire to be secure, the desire to have permanency—is burned away at the root? Can we discover that for ourselves, not because someone else has talked about it, and be aware of it directly, so that the very root, the very desire to be secure and to have permanency is burned away?

This desire to have permanency, either of the future or the past, to hold on to the accumulation of experience, gives one the sense of security. Can that be burned away? It is that which creates conditioning. The desire to know, which most of us have, and in that very knowing to find security, to have experience, which gives us strength—can we wipe all that away? Not by volition, but burn it away in awareness so that the mind is free from all its desires. Then that which is eternal can come into being.

That is the only revolution, not the communist or any other form of revolution. They do not solve our problems; on the contrary, they increase them; they multiply our sorrows. Surely the only true revolution is freeing the mind from its own conditioning, and therefore from society—not the mere reformation of society. The one who reforms society is still caught in society, but the one who is free of society, being free from conditioning, will act in their own way, which will act again upon society.

So our problem is not reformation, how to improve society, how to have a better welfare state, or what you will. It is not an economic or political revolution, or peace through terror. For one who is serious, these are not the problems. The real problem is to find out whether the mind can be totally free from all conditioning and thereby perhaps discover in that extraordinary silence that which is beyond all measurement.

The real revolution is inward

The real revolution is inward, and it comes into being without the mind seeking it. What the mind seeks and finds, however reasonable, however rational and intelligent, is never the final answer. For the mind is put together, and what it creates is also put together; therefore it can be undone. But the revolution of which I am speaking is the truly religious life, stripped of all the absurdities of organized religions throughout the world. It has nothing to do with priests, with symbols, with churches.

You cannot co-operate if you are not alone

A religious mind is a mind that is completely alone. Aloneness is not isolation; it is the actual state of cooperation. You cannot cooperate if you are not alone.

Generally, you only cooperate when there is a reward or punishment, when you are getting something, when you want to do something together under an authority or under the umbrella of ideas. When you are working for a utopia or an ideal, you are really not cooperating; the idea attracts you and you are absorbed by the idea. When you disagree with the idea, you break away. That is what is happening with all the communities: in this utopia, an ideal society, everybody is against another! The communist world is like that too. Though they started out to have an idealistic, utopian world, the competition became more brutal, more ruthless, and they are all trying to cooperate with the state—communes, collective farms, forcing people to cooperate, and therefore inwardly battling, destroying, looking for ways and means where you can go against all this. That is not cooperation.

Cooperation only comes when you are alone. There is this sense of complete aloneness, which is the natural outcome of a mind that has no escapes, no fear, no authority, and has understood the whole problem of energy. Then it is in a state of cooperation. And therefore, being in a state of cooperation, it also knows when not to cooperate.

9

HOW DOES THE FREE MIND LIVE IN THIS WORLD?

Krishnamurti: As long as the mind is caught in the stream of memory, pleasant or unpleasant, as long as it is held in the chain of cause-effect, as long as it is using the present as a passage from the past to the future, it can never be free. Freedom is then merely an idea, not an actuality. The truth of this must be seen, and then your question will have quite a different significance.

Question: If I see the truth of it, will there be freedom?

Krishnamurti: Speculation is vain. The truth must be seen: the actual fact that there is no freedom as long as the mind is a prisoner of the past.

Has one who is free, in this ultimate sense, any relationship to the stream of causation and time? If not, then what is the good of this freedom? What value or significance has such a person in this world of joy and pain? It is strange how we nearly always think in terms of utility. Are you not asking this question from a boat adrift on the stream of time? And from there you want to know what significance a free person has for the people in the boat. Probably none at all.

Most people are not interested in freedom, and when they meet one who is free, they either make of them a deity and place them in a shrine, or they put them away in stone or words—which is to destroy them. But surely your concern is not with such a person. Your concern is with freeing the mind of the past—the mind that is you.

§

Question: Once the mind is free, then what is its responsibility?

Krishnamurti: The word responsibility is not applicable to such a mind. Its very existence has an explosive action on time, on the past. It is this explosive action that is of the highest importance. The one who remains in the boat and asks for help wants it in the pattern of the past, in the field of recognition, and to this the free mind has no reply. But that explosive freedom acts on the bondage of time.

10

THE INTELLIGENCE THAT BRINGS ORDER AND PEACE

Most of us are trying to solve the many difficulties we have within the artificial distinction created between the group and the individual. To me, such a distinction as the individual opposed to the group perverts thinking and destroys clarity of thought, leading to repression and exaggeration, which must exist between the individual and the group.

As we search for ways and means out of this chaos, clever and complicated methods and solutions are offered, with each individual choosing according to their idiosyncrasy and fancy, depending on their upbringing, social class or their religion. I do not want to add any new ideas, theories or explanations to the already existing theories, but the real solution to any problem lies through intelligence, which must be direct and simple. When there is such intelligence, we can understand life as a whole. Intelligence is not to be awakened by following any group or by obeying one's idiosyncrasies and fancies.

To understand what intelligence is, we must first inquire into the many stupidities that cripple the mind and heart. We are not asking what intelligence is, because in freeing the mind from stupidity through constant alertness, we shall then be able to know what intelligence is itself. In this process of awakening intelligence, that is, seeking and trying to find out the limitations that our environment has placed about us, and stripping those, sloughing off those stupidities, we shall begin to realize what true intelligence is.

We have many ideas about the richness, completeness and immortality of life. But the richness and completeness of life can only be understood when the mind is completely free from the limitations, stupidities and idiosyncrasies that circumstances and environment, of the past or the present, inherited or acquired, are continually placing about us.

Each party, each expert, each authority offers a way out of this increasing conflict. Each puts forward an idea, a theory, a system toward the solution of this terrifying tangle. We can divide these theorists, these people who give explanations, into two types: those who offer explanations from the point of view of turning outward and those who offer explanations turned inward.

The expert turned outward says that the majority of human problems can be controlled, shaped, corrected by controlling the environment. They say human thought can be changed, altered, controlled through organization, whether the organization of work, the means of production and distribution, and so forth. They regard human beings as clay, as matter to be conditioned by environment. If we can control that environment, in the perfection of the group, the individual will have the opportunity to express themselves. They can be conditioned according to a new set of ideas so that they never come, as an individual, in conflict with the group or society.

If you think that a human being is nothing else but matter to be so conditioned, there is nothing more to be said. Then it is very simple: let us all work for the perfection of the environment, bringing about new theories and new ideas, and condition our mind to that. I am not against or for it, but I want to go into it more fully. That is, if a human being is merely a social entity and by altering circumstances and environment, and creating in them the habit of social wellbeing so that they shall not be antisocial—if that is all then it seems life becomes very shallow and superficial, a series of unfulfilled, chaotic, superficial actions.

Then you have the person who, being turned inward, says that life is nothing but spirit. Leave it to the highest in humanity and follow the highest laid down by teachers and philosophical systems; let them become more religious, let them follow the various teachers, let them have greater discipline, prayers, organizations of a spiritual kind, let them obey authority, let them be led by fear, psychological promptings and spiritual guides so that they will conquer circumstances and environment.

So, you have the exaggerations of the person turned outward and the exaggerations of the person turned inward. That is, on the one hand, someone who says humanity is nothing but matter and therefore to be conditioned perpetually through environment; and on the other, someone turned inward, the so-called spiritual, who exaggerates the moral, the away-from-matter. One says environment first, the other says spirit first. In their exaggeration and emphasis, they destroy their own ends. Whereas the true solution, or rather the true manner of thought that awakens intelligence, lies in the perfect equilibrium between the two. In that equilibrium, which is true intelligence, lies the simple and direct way of solving the problem of our innumerable social and individual conflicts.

To really study the various systems, philosophical and economic, to be able to study them all thoroughly, to be able to compare, requires time. Few have the capacity or inclination to penetrate their complicated reasoning and theories. So what happens when you haven't time to inquire into the explanations of innumerable competing experts? We choose one whom we like, who looks reasonable. As we haven't time to go into it thoroughly, we accept their authority. The greater the expert, the greater the authority, the greater the following. So, as usual, gradually the followers become blind and follow dogmas, and then what happens? The followers destroy the leaders, and the leaders destroy the followers. Gradually we create another set of stupidities under the set of dogmas which were originally theories, and we become slave to them.

Take religion, that is, religion as an organized belief, and you will see that the authority of the expert is supreme. The pattern is set out, and you are forced by opinion, through fear, through the pressure of public opinion and so forth, to follow. That pressure is exerted, and you are forced to follow. This worship of authority, this worship of the expert without knowing their limitations, is the very root of exploitation.

So, the whole process of living, which should be a continual fulfilment and therefore a continual penetration into reality, into what is true, is wholly destroyed through this worship of authority, of specialists, of dogmas, creeds and theories. The whole process makes the individual subservient, makes them obey and follow. So, we gradually become unconscious to everything but the pattern and live as much as we can in the edicts of that pattern, and we call that living.

Our environment becomes only the mould to shape the individual. The individual then, as now, is nothing else but an exaggeration, the exaggerated expression of environment—environment being the past and the present, the inherited and the acquired. That is, the individual whom we call "I" is nothing else but the expression of that environment.

So, we are conditioned by environment. You are the result of your past and present environment, and what you express, what you call individuality, is nothing but that environment. There are very few who are capable of freeing themselves from environment and expressing that. But the true expression of individuality is that intelligence that is awakened through freeing the mind from the environment of the past and the present. So there is only intelligence when the
mind understands the significance through constant awareness of the environment.

Groups merely impose another set of further stupidities, further limitations. Systems are but the crystallization of thoughts, and groups are the expression of that thought. So can these crystallized thoughts, and following them, awaken intelligence, or have you to begin not considering yourself as an individual or as part of a group, but penetrate into the stupidities of the group and the environment? That is to think anew, so as to be able to question, so as to be able to discover the true significance of each environment, each limitation.

If we cannot be so active, emotionally and mentally, the mere following of a system, and being active in that system, does not create or awaken intelligence. It is by continual and constant questioning of environment that you can free the mind from the many stupidities which those environments have imposed. To do that, we must look at the problem not from the point of view of the individual or the group, but from the point of view of what is true.

Now, such intelligence, when it is awakened, can truly cooperate, not with stupidities but with other intelligences. Take, for instance, what is happening with regard to war. To find out about the stupidity of war, we must think, right from the beginning, not from the nationalistic, racial or class point of view at all. Inherently, war is wrong. There is no excuse for war so long as intelligence is functioning. But as politicians rule us, the majority of them stupid, we are led from war to war, and there are innumerable reasons given for a defensive war or an aggressive war.

As long as you do not think clearly, fundamentally, from the very beginning with regard to this question, one day you will be for peace, and another day you will be for war because you are not at the point where you have discovered fundamentally the appalling cruelties, the racial hatreds, the exploitations that exist and which create war. Only when there is an awakened intelligence, not only on your part but on the part of politicians and rulers, will there be peace.

To discover what is true requires great intelligence. Intelligence is not book knowledge. You can read many, many books and yet be colossally stupid. You can read a great many philosophies and yet not know what creative thinking is. The mind begins to free itself through constant awareness of the stupidities it is creating for itself or has acquired. The whole purpose of thought and emotion is, after all, to find out what is true. When you have discovered what is true, there is true intelligence.

Can anyone else tell you what is true? Can anyone tell you what God is? I don't think anyone can; you have to find out for yourself. To find out what is true, what the significance of life is, what immortality is, you must have intelligence. Without that, life becomes a chaotic triviality. Therefore, to awaken that intelligence, we must strip the mind of stupidities.

The first cause of stupidity is our consciousness, from which innumerable causes of stupidity and action arise. That is, this consciousness that clings to the particular, and so creates the distinction between the group and the individual, this consciousness that sings, "My"—my progress, my house, my family, my growth, my ambition—that consciousness is the very root of the limitations that cripple thought.

One of its manifestations is the fundamental craving for security, security in the realm of one's entire being, security physically, emotionally and mentally. That security is what we want. In the search for security, there is bound to be conflict between what we call the individual and the group—the exaggerations of the individual as against the group, and therefore the conflict. This search for security expresses itself in possessions, cruelty, exploitation, and the terrifying stupidities of wars, nationalism and racial hatred.

Emotionally, love has become but possessiveness. Love is no longer a creative joy. It is a series of conflicts and battles. Its ecstasies are destroyed because through it all runs this desire for possessiveness. Then you have the desire to be certain. That is why we so worship authority, the great teachers. That is why we go to so-called spiritual meetings, to try to find out if there is an ultimate end so that we can cling to it. That is why the constant inquiry into truth and God. And we worship the person who assures us there is a God, or that there is immortality, because it gives us comfort and security. Gradually this worship of security destroys intelligence as when we, through experience, begin to accumulate memories. That memory functioning continually prevents our adjustment and adaptability to the constant movement of life.

Take, for example, what happens when you have had an experience you have not fully understood. The memory of it continues, and with that memory you meet the next experience. So you rely on memory for the understanding, fruition and completeness of that experience. You do not come to it free, full of freshness. So experience is continually creating memory, and with that memory you meet life. It must naturally act as a barrier. As physically we seek security, we move mentally from certainty to certainty, with never a moment of complete despair.

I assure you that when there is complete nakedness, utter hopelessness, you will find in that moment of non-security, of absolute uncertainty and therefore continual search and inquiry, something much greater than security or certainty.

While there is the search for security, fear arises, which gradually begets many illusions, false self-discipline, suppressions, limitations, the fear of death, and the inquiry into the hereafter. We are interested in the hereafter because our life is so superficial, conditioned by environment, conflicting, appalling, chaotic, unreasonable, without joy and without ecstasy. So we look to the future, and therefore there is fear of death. To me, immortality is a continual becoming, not of that consciousness which we call the "I", but that consciousness which is freed from the particular as well as the group, that consciousness that creates the distinction. That is, the mind is stripped of all stupidities and is therefore able to perceive the continued thought which is ever becoming. But that is a thing you cannot explain, you cannot reason about, you cannot talk about. It has to be experienced. It has to be lived. To do that, one requires persistency and constant purposefulness. So, the state of the world, the chaos caused by the conflict of many theories, leading to stupid practices and divisions, and the accumulating knowledge of theories, leads to increasingly bitter divisions, creating mass movements for conflicting experiments. We are immersed in conflict, and intelligence, which is the true expression and mode of life, is wholly forgotten.

We see this, and what should be our action? What should be our attitude, our thought? That is, are you going to wait for the perfection of environment through revolution, through economic changes, through political upheaval? This waiting is to lose yourself in illusion, which is but escaping to hope. Or, will you begin not as individuals, not as groups, but begin to think anew so that you shake off the many stupidities that have become virtues, so many things that we have taken for granted or accepted, so that you can think directly and simply from the very beginning?

Which are you going to do, wait for the future, hoping that environment will be perfected through a miracle, through somebody's action, or become aware so intensely, because you are yourself in conflict with environment and circumstances, that you stop all escapes? That is the very essence of intelligence, in which there is no possibility of an escape, so that you see directly and simply.

That is the problem: to penetrate into the conditions and environment so that we see this true significance and not create a new set of stupidities, a new set of illusions. And therefore we bring about clarity of thought and therefore clarity of action. Or do we merely wait, marking time, which leads to utter disorder, superficiality, to boredom, to the superficial lives most people lead, whether in the intensity of work or lack of work? Go to any place, to any party, to the innumerable theatres, and you will see the superficiality of life. I am not condemning theatres because I go there myself.

You see what is happening more and more: there is despair, waiting for action, waiting for governments to act. And in the meantime, our own lives are becoming superficial, shallow. Therefore we have the inanities of modern society and modern spiritual people, searching for guides and so forth.

So, intelligence is the only solution that makes for real harmony of action between mind and heart, between real affection and thought. No system, no alteration of environment from the outside is ever going to give human beings the true ecstasy of expression or of life.

SOURCES

INTRODUCTION
United Nations Talk, 11 April 1985

CHAPTER 1
Paris Talk 1, 16 April 1968

CHAPTER 2
It must be fairly obvious...
Madras Talk 1, 11 January 1956

In all our relationships...
Madras Talk 3, 5 February 1950

We realize that there must be a fundamental change...
Madanapalle Talk 2, 19 February 1956

Because we have created this society...
Bombay Talk 1, 10 February 1965

We must realize that the world's problem...
Bangalore Talk 2, 11 July 1948

At whatever level you live...
Colombo Talk 2, 1 January 1950

Question: You say that, fundamentally, my mind...
Brockwood Park Q&A 2, 2 September 1980

Question: How can the idea that you are the world...
Saanen Q&A 1, 21 July 1981

As an individual, it is your responsibility...
Bombay Talk 1, 10 February 1965

CHAPTER 3
Without a radical transformation...
New Delhi Talk 4, 18 February 1959

Life is a complex problem...
Madras Talk 2, 26 October 1947

It must be fairly obvious to most of us...
Bombay Talk 6, 14 March 1950

As society exists now...
Bombay Talk 2, 14 February 1965

The Social patterns is set up by humanity...
Commentaries on Living, Series 3

You are responsible for the condition...
Bombay Talk 7, 3 March 1965

CHAPTER 4
Question: Since the major causes of catastrophe...
Ojai Talk 2, 2 June 1940

Question: How can individual regeneration alone...
Madras Talk 8, 27 January 1952

Question: Can I, religiously inclined...
Madras Talk 5, 19 January 1952

Question: One sees chaos in the world...
Saanen Q&A 1, 29 July 1981

Question: Why don't you participate in politics...
Colombo Talk 4, 15 January 1950

Question: Why don't you face the economic...
Ojai Talk 7, 25 June 1944

Question: Why do you waste your time...
Colombo Talk 2, 1 January 1950

If the reformer, the contributor...
Ojai Talk 7, 8 July 1945

The problem is this: a mind that is not innocent...
New Delhi Discussion 6, 20 January 1961

CHAPTER 5
Question: All except a few do not want war...
Benares Talk 3, 17 December 1967

As long as we use technological knowledge...
New Delhi Radio Talk, 6 November 1948

To have peace, you must live peacefully...
Bombay Talk 6, 28 February 1965

Is this vast problem of the world your problem...
Benares Talk 1, 16 January 1949

Question: Are individuals impotent...
Benares Talk 1, 9 January 1955

Question: Will there be an end to these evil wars...
Benares Talk 1, 10 December 1967

Question: Don't you think there are peace-loving nations...
Ojai Talk 7, 25 June 1944

We know that war is the process of history...
Saanen Talk 5, 19 July 1966

Your own mind is conditioned...
New York Talk 2, 23 May 1954

The prevention of ever-increasing destruction...
Ojai Talk 10, 16 July 1944

CHAPTER 6
Do you notice nature...
Bombay Discussion 22, 6 March 1948

What is human nature...
Ojai Talk 6, 23 June 1934

Relationship between people...
Bombay Discussion 25, 18 March 1948

Question: Why is it that in the balance of nature...
Brockwood Q&A 2, 4 September 1980

Question: The whole world of nature...
Ojai Q&A 2, 16 May 1985

CHAPTER 7
I do not know why we educate our children...
Ojai Discussion 3, 12 April 1977

What happens when you have been through the mill...
Benares Talk 1, 8 November 1956

Education is the capacity to help you...
Benares Talk 3, 20 November 1956

CHAPTER 8
The future of humanity is at stake...
Calcutta Talk 1, 20 November 1982

What is the responsibility of a human being...
San Diego Conversation 4, 19 February 1974

Unless there is a change…
Bombay Talk 2, 16 February 1966

It is not a revolution within oneself…
Saanen Talk 4, 18 July 1965

Question: What effect does a revolution…
New York Talk 6, 7 October 1966

Question: What you are really telling us…
London Talk 4, 7 May 1966

Is it possible for there to be no conflict at all…
Ojai Talk 2, 3 April 1977

Can we consider this…
London Talk 1, 17 June 1955

The real revolution is inward…
Brussels Talk 6, 25 June 1956

A religious mind…
Madras Talk 7, 2 February 1964

CHAPTER 9
Question: Once the mind is free…
Commentaries On Living, Series 3

CHAPTER 10
New York Talk 1, 11 March 1935